THE PLAYS OF THORNTON WILDER
A Critical Study

THE PLAYS OF

THORNTON WILDER

A Critical Study

BY

DONALD HABERMAN

WESLEYAN UNIVERSITY PRESS

Middletown, Connecticut

Library of Congress Catalog Card Number: 67 – 15772

Manufactured in the United States of America

First Edition

To Lidia Wachsler Haberman

What good is it for a man to be dissatisfied with always repeating the same acts? For he must, just like the animals, perform and repeat daily those acts which are basic and indispensable to life, if he does not wish to die.

— LUIGI PIRANDELLO

CONTENTS

ACKNOWLEDGMENTS

PERMISSION has very kindly been given me by Mr. Thornton Wilder to quote from "The American Loneliness," *Atlantic*, 190 (July 1952): 29–37; *The Angel That Troubled the Waters;* "Emily Dickinson," *Atlantic*, 190 (Nov. 1952): 65–69; the Introduction to *Jacob's Dream;* "James Joyce," *Poetry, A Magazine of Verse,* 57 (Mar. 1941): 370–374; "Joyce and the Modern Novel," *A James Joyce Miscellany,* n.p., 1957, pp. 11–19; *Lucrece; The Merchant of Yonkers;* "Noting the Nature of Farce"; the Introduction to *Oedipus the King,* tr. Francis Storr; "A Preface to 'Our Town' "; "Some Thoughts on Playwriting," *The Intent of the Artist,* Princeton, 1941; "Thoughts for Our Time," *Harvard Alumni Bulletin,* 53 (July 7, 1951): 779–781; "A Time of Troubles," in *Academy Papers,* New York, 1951; "The Trumpet Shall Sound," in four successive issues of the *Yale Literary Magazine,* 85 (Oct. 1919–Jan. 1920); "The Warship," *Yale Literary Magazine,* 101 (Feb. 1936): 64–67; "World Literature and the Modern Mind," *Goethe and the Modern Age,* Chicago, 1950.

From the following manuscripts: "The Alcestiad"; "Author's suggestions for staging the play," Yale Library Collection of American Literature; "Memo on second half of Act I 'The Skin of Our Teeth' "; "Our Town," first full manuscript, Yale Library Collection of American Literature; "L'Oeuvre et le langage"; "Sloth: the Wreck on the Five-Twenty-Five"; *The Woman of Andros,* Yale Library Collection of American Literature.

From a letter to Mrs. G. P. Baker, March 1938; a letter to Max Reinhardt; a quotation from a letter to Tallulah Bankhead quoted in a letter from Tallulah Bankhead to Michael Meyerberg, Oct. 28, 1942, all in the Yale Library Collection of American Literature.

The epigraphs to the chapters of this book are all from Thornton Wilder; in order, *The Ides of March;* from "Novelist into Playwright," *Saturday Review of Literature;* "Thoughts for Our Time," *Harvard Alumni Bulletin;* "Some Thoughts on Playwriting," *The Intent of the Artist;* "The Art of Fiction XVI," *Paris Review.*

I wish to thank James Doehler, Donald Gallup of the Yale Library, George Pistorius, Dr. Stella Wachsler, William W. Watt, and my wife.

And especially a debt of gratitude is owed to Francis Fergusson, who first revealed to me the "Idea of a Theater"; to Professor Norman Holmes Pearson, who guided this book from its beginning as a dissertation at Yale University to its present form and who offered in friendship his intelligence, knowledge, wit, and good humor; to Miss Isabel Wilder, who generously and kindly provided me with information along with her judgment and good will; and to Mr. Thornton Wilder, who graciously and patiently answered endless questions and permitted me to read manuscripts of his work.

THE PLAYS OF THORNTON WILDER
A Critical Study

PREFACE:
EVERYBODY'S THORNTON WILDER

AS a young man traveling in Europe, Thornton Wilder confessed with rueful humor in a letter to a friend back home that he found it necessary to appear disguised in order to be recognized. Although Arnold Bennett had already proclaimed to his readers the discovery of a new American writer, Wilder was not having trouble playing a role created by publicity. His sole concern was to acquire all the proper clothes needed to explore English society, where indeed he would not have been recognized even as existing had he not been got up in the correct costume. Today Wilder's role is a different one. As a successful novelist and playwright, he commands attention on his own. His plays are sponsored abroad by the State Department. He wins prizes. He is invited to the White House by two successive administrations, though presidential recognition is an ambiguous symbol of artistic arrival. The New York *Times* reports his frequent moves, retailing all it can collect from steamship and airline personnel. Wilder is a man of some public interest, even beyond the horizons of the literary world. But if the propriety of his costume matters less, considerable curiosity is still aroused by the details of his disguises. This book will disappoint that curiosity.

The cult of personality is powerful in our time. Many of the famous thrive on the worship of an audience; they create publicity and live exposed. In spite of the truth behind the image of the artist as an exile, writers are not exempt from the pitfalls of fame. Ernest Hemingway, as he himself describes it in *A Moveable Feast,* is only one pitiful example of the dissolution of private living under the pressures of competing with a self created to satisfy the inane hungers of the public. Wilder, in contrast, is an elusive figure, dodging his critics as well as his admirers, always just slipping away in silence. If his decision to retire to the Arizona desert was reported with fanfare in every newspaper across the country, he nonetheless virtually disappeared from view for almost two years, returning only to receive the Presidential Medal in December, 1963.

As I began this book on a living writer who officially, at least, lived nearby, the advantages of personally discussing his work with him gleamed remotely ahead. I wanted to know the man who had written *The Skin of Our Teeth*. But the artist was not in residence; I first met his sister, Miss Isabel Wilder, instead.

Since the beginning of World War II when she resigned her own career as novelist, Miss Wilder has stood as buffer between her brother and the pestering world. She answers the letters of school children who write to *Thorton* Wilder to know by next Tuesday please what Emily's death means. She politely deals with aspiring writers who want aid, financial or otherwise. She watches with a shrewd eye over all major productions of the plays. From the point of view of the student and critic, Miss Wilder is obviously in a unique and extraordinary position vis-à-vis her brother's work. As for facts, she knows virtually everything, and with exceptional kindness she agreed to supply answers to my endless questions. She also made available to me her enormously interesting but incredibly small collection of Wilderiana; it is small because Wilder keeps virtually nothing and Miss Wilder must salvage what she can. My meeting with Miss Wilder was therefore in no way disappointing. Through talking with her and through reading notes, unpublished writing, and some correspondence, I was drawing nearer, I thought, to the man himself. I would confront him personally for the first time when he returned to his home.

I remember waiting for him on a hot, still summer afternoon in New Haven; his arrival was a shock to the quiet and a surprise to my imaginary acquaintance with the man. While I had never subscribed to the nonsense of the kindly teacher — though he is a teacher and he is kind — that has for want of a more specific public character accumulated around him, neither had I expected so grand a blast of energy. And though he is forcefully alive, this picture of Wilder is both true and false, like the notion of the kindly teacher; for the impression I have always taken away from my meetings with him is that he is an exceptionally quick observer and, as Henry James would have it, deep.

He is interested, although not absorbed, in everything around him, from his new suit — Isn't it wonderful? It's drip-dry! — to Antonioni's latest movie. But while I was presumably going to learn about him, he began sharply to question me: What music did I prefer? What languages did I speak? Read? What did I *do*? Somewhat uneasily I felt I was failing and passing, too, I hoped, a set of swift tests, none of which revealed my "personality," but all of which served to expose the strengths together with the inadequacies of my mind. I began to examine myself, rather than Wilder, and I supposed weakly that perhaps really I did not *do* anything, in the sense that I harbored no secret ambitions to compose symphonies. And that brought us to what genuinely appeared to attract his unwavering interest: his craft, his own writing.

Though Wilder tells wonderful stories and anecdotes peopled with the famous and near famous, he talks seldom *directly* about himself. His liveliness is never mere tattle, for the point of his talk is inevitably intellectual, and just as inevitably it relates to himself, to his work. Sometimes the significance of his apparent subject to his real one is not immediately clear, but it is there, and it manifests itself for the patient listener. His refusal to speak of himself openly is complemented by an overt modesty, sometimes coy but always humorous. He protested that books about his work ought to wait for his death, and he seemed mildly amused at the prospect of a study of his plays. Though he seemed very sensitive to what he considered stupid or unfair criticism of his work and spoke of his entertaining me as "payola" for a favorable book, ultimately I'm sure he dismisses the attitude of a professional critic toward his work as irrelevant.

But what did I learn about Thornton Wilder himself? There are facts. Along with a twin brother who was stillborn, he was born in 1897, in Madison, Wisconsin, and the family remained in Madison long enough for him to begin school there. When his father was appointed American Consul General in Hong Kong, he went along and was put for a short time as a day student in one of the two monstrous German schools the Wilder children attended during part of their China stay. Wilder's sister still remembers with horror spending hours filling up the squares of graph paper with neat circles and having her *cahier* trampled before the class under the feet of the former army-officer teacher as a punishment for making a mistake in her lesson. Before finally graduating from the Berkeley High School in California in 1915, Wilder went for varying lengths of time and with inter-ruptions to another German school; the English China Inland Mission School at Cheefoo; the Thatcher School at Ojai, California; and, of course, the Berkeley public schools. The Wilder children were moved rapidly about (Miss Wilder was never in attendance in June, so that she did not formally graduate from anywhere). Wilder's autocratic father chose Oberlin College for him largely because of its religious emphasis and because he wanted Thornton to have the experience of attending a coeducational college. Continuing the variety of his sec-ondary education, however, after two years Wilder transferred to his father's alma mater, Yale. He interrupted his Yale days with eight months with the First Coast Artillery at Fort Adams in Rhode Island during World War I, separating from the army as a corporal to return to Yale to graduate in 1920. By this time his family was living in New Haven, where from the success of *The Bridge of San Luis Rey* some years later he eventually built a house, still known as the "house the *Bridge* built."

Following Yale, Wilder went to Europe. There he resided at the American Academy in Rome and began writing his first published novel, *The Cabala*. His father recalled him with a position to teach French at the Lawrenceville School, and he thus began a teaching career that led him to the University of Chicago and to a year at Har-vard, with short stopovers to lecture at various places here and abroad. In between he found time to earn an M.A. at Princeton. During World War II, he would surely have been exempt from military duty, but believing that what is worth having is worth fighting for, he vol-unteered for the Army Air Force and was accepted into Intelligence; when he was separated at the close of the war he had achieved the rank of Lieutenant Colonel. Presently he has finished a novel, *The Eighth Day,* his first in almost twenty years, to be published in the spring of 1967.

Dull as these facts are, they are not utterly unyielding. It is dramatically apparent that as a child Wilder had no home in the sense that he never lived long enough in any one place to become attached to a particular region and its rhythm of life. His education is wildly various. His experience is the American experience exaggerated, and he has continued his early way of life, constantly and restlessly traveling. Even now he has no family of his own, but carries with him the memory of his childhood family and especially of his mother.

Characteristically no gossip has attached itself to him, and he is a man who has lived actively in the literary, theatrical, and international social worlds, which are not known for either their charity or the silence of their tongues. Although he knows an enormous number of people, close and devoted friends and acquaintances, to the eyes of the world there has been no obvious and apparent sustained intimacy with another human being, except certainly with his sister, with Gertrude Stein, and perhaps with Lady Sybil Colefax. And even with them he has managed an admirable privacy not easy to establish and maintain. When his correspondence and Gertrude Stein's, too, are published, the curious will discover more about Wilder's personal life.

Perhaps because he is a wanderer, Wilder lives free from human acquisitiveness. His carelessness about his own effects was vividly dramatized while I was working on those papers Wilder has unsystematically managed to keep. At that time an enormous quantity of material belonging to an American writer who had just died was moving into the Yale Collection of American Literature (ironically the writer was a Harvard alumnus) and dispossessing almost everything else until it could be sorted and catalogued. Later I learned that, moved by the generosity of the moment and an incurable urge to improve the minds of those he meets, Wilder gave away to a young lady at the time he was working on *The Skin of Our Teeth* a copy of *Finnegans Wake* in which he had been making notes. Though Wilder still has in his possession what he considers to be "THE copy" of Joyce's book, it would be extremely useful to students of his life work to have this other as well. His study, the only room in his house truly his, is quite bare. Strange for a scholar — and he is a good one — he keeps very few books: his treasured sets of Lope de Vega, Shakespeare, Joyce, and the great nineteenth-century American writers Whitman, Emily Dickinson, Thoreau, Poe, and Melville. Always having lived near a large university, he depends on libraries, unlike his 1928 European walking-tour companion, Gene Tunney, about whom it is humorously reported that he kept adding the books that cropped up in Wilder's talk to his knapsack until it became unbearably heavy. All Wilder's books exist inside himself, where he makes them truly his own.

If the volumes themselves are relatively unimportant to Wilder, what they contain is not. Most writers get what they know from the life around them, through participation and sharp observation. Although Wilder knows people and is constantly interviewing them and learning about them, by his own admission he respects the individual's right to privacy. His inspiration for the story in his writing frequently comes from the work of others — novels, plays, and letters — or completely from his imagination. His knowledge of the people around him quickens and heightens his reading to make what he finds there new. Perhaps clouded by the image of Sunday School and high-school productions of *Our Town,* the precision and brilliance of Wilder's mind — all finally, I think, that can matter to his readers — are frequently obscured. It is important to remember that the other art that most interests Wilder is the most abstract and removed of all: music.

It may be that this characteristic retirement of Wilder's artistic personality and human personality as well has led him to be so fascinated with the theater, for playwriting is the most impersonal kind of literary performance. In its greatest achievement, the author's voice and personality are everywhere alike and at the same time nowhere, in that the plot and action are their own comment and no one character is the spokesman for the author. Keenly aware of this, Wilder said:

> A dramatist is one who believes that the pure event, an action involving human beings, is more arresting than any comment that can be made upon it. . . . A novel is what *took place;* no self-effacement on the

part of the narrator can hide the fact that we hear his voice recounting, recalling events . . . which he has selected . . . to lay before us from his presiding intelligence.

[Drama is] Experience for experience's sake.[1]

He added, "I regard the theater as the greatest of all art forms."

Wilder, who in his novels has tended toward didacticism, sees his plays as a place where comment and didactic intentions are held at a minimum, and (until he wrote *The Ides of March*) he considered his plays his best work. What, then, can the audience know of the playwright? The total play itself characterizes, not the playwright's emotions and passions, but his mind, his intellect. "The most powerful weapon of an author [for the stage] is his mind,"[2] Richard Boleslavsky has written, and in these terms Wilder seems eminently suited to write plays, for he is an extraordinarily intellectual person, not only in that he is concerned with what is usually understood or misunderstood as the intellectual life but also in that he is identifiable, not by his disguises of ordinary living defined by his relations wth other people, but by his very exceptional and powerful mind existing alone.

And in the list of facts, of special significance is his teaching career. He has always been passionately devoted to reaching the minds of other people. Teachers have been described as bad actors; they perform before an audience, and at their best they dazzle with the mind, not by personality. Wilder is also an actor, but not a bad one; indeed, he is a very good one — on stage and off also. He is an exceptionally amusing and charming man. His disguises, for he does have them, are successful ones, and he has had much experience and time to perfect them as he wandered everywhere meeting and talking with everyone — from Texas Guinan to Lady Cunard (perhaps not such a far journey!). His social manner is of a time past: it has nothing to do with what he is thinking, but it is not unnatural. He is almost courtly. At the conclusion to the introduction to the *Three Plays* he wrote, "And as I view the work of my contemporaries I seem to feel that I am exceptional in one thing — I give (don't I?) the impression of having enormously enjoyed it." He does give the "impression," but that is not the same thing — and the sentence suggests, perhaps, that it is — as actually having done it. Wilder is here describing the tone of the finished work: the lingering illusion is that he has described himself. To know Thornton Wilder is to agree with his comment on his work. He gives the impression of enjoying himself enormously, and therefore he is a very satisfying man to be with. But the nagging word *impression* remains, for he is an actor (except, perhaps, when he talks about writing), and I feel that I do not know what an interview might describe as the *real* Thornton Wilder at all.

I have been trying to say that Wilder's mind is available in his work to all who would grasp it. For the rest, he is a very private man, though, as he says of himself, an obliging man, and he willingly talks with all who will listen. He once described his ambition to be the Poet Laureate of Coney Island. I think his ambition is fulfilled. His writing describes the living of all Americans without respect for individualizing and separating characteristics. But that is the point: it is everybody's life. As an individual man with particularizing details, Wilder disappears into the crowd, and only his mind and skill separate him from the crowd. In this book I have respected Wilder's privacy; indeed, I think his human biography is not especially relevant to an examination of his work, for his work is the biography of his mind.

—D. H.

Missoula, Montana
October 1966

I

THE SAVOR OF LIFE

They think that by evading ... death's contemplation they
are enhancing the savor of life. The reverse is true;
only those who have grasped their non-being are
capable of praising the sunlight.

THORNTON WILDER does not, in the traditional way, demonstrate his attitude toward life in the process of telling a story; his attitude toward life is his story. The stance Wilder has assumed is to display the essential flavor and overwhelming value in living itself. His work, from its beginnings, though it then lacked the power and the clarity of his later plays and novels, struggled with remarkable persistency to force the attention of the audience on "the savor of life," as he puts it, through "death's contemplation." The development in Wilder's work has not been so much on what he wanted to say as on finding an adequate way to say it. Ultimately, of course, his ideas were deepened and strengthened also.

When he first began writing as a child, Wilder made up plays to be acted out by himself, his friends, and his sisters. Though pretending and play acting are the stuff of every childhood, they are usually put away with other childish games; Wilder, however, never stopped writing plays. While at Oberlin and then at Yale in the years 1915–1920 he had the pleasure of seeing some of his early pieces published in the undergraduate magazines and then later in *S4N,* one of the "little magazines" of the early twenties, edited by recent Yale graduates. He collected in 1928 seventeen of these early plays in one volume, *The Angel That Troubled the Waters,* which was one of the first books on the list of the newly formed publishing house of Coward-McCann, one of whose partners, Thomas R. Coward, had also been at Yale with Wilder. All these plays are short, the longest being about seventeen pages, and Wilder appropriately called them Three Minute Plays. Except, perhaps, for the kind of closet performance given them in the living room of Frank Walls, who taught at the Yale Art School, they were intended only to be read, for they are, except in form, not really plays at all.

Wilder wrote the Three Minute Plays surprisingly under the direct inspiration of a little-known book by Theodore Dreiser called *Plays of the Natural and the Supernatural*. Though one ordinarily thinks of Dreiser and his powerful version of naturalism as being far from Wilder's careful style, Wilder so admired this collection of plays, which had been published in 1916, that in the ornamental border of a bookplate he designed for himself when he was at Oberlin, he incorporated Dreiser's name along with his other enthusiasms of that time, which extended from the actress Elsie Ferguson to the music of Mozart. The plays in Dreiser's strange little book are a kind of combination of symbolist and expressionist dramas and, like Wilder's plays, were never intended for the stage. The normally unspoken thoughts of the characters are expressed simultaneously with action, much of which is purely hallucinatory or outside the *mise en scène* proper. Little or no attempt is made to represent the shock and new perception of two or more particular people confronting one another. Dreiser depended instead on artificial symbols burdened with obscure meanings, and all the elements in the plays are made to cohere and are given whatever vitality they possess by the mood and expressed intention, rather than by facts and action.

As a young man Wilder naturally was attracted to writing that promised a great depth of meaning and demanded so little payment in the coin of formal discipline. The Three Minute Plays appear profound because their shadowy but really simple mystery is disguised by Wilder's so exceptionally careful writing.

But not only Dreiser's free and undemanding form attracted Wilder's imagination; his ideas did as well. In Dreiser's play *The Spring Recital* various spirits of priests, a Minister of St. Giles, Three Priests of Isis, and a Monk of the Thebaid, during an organ recital congregate in the upper reaches of a church in an American city. There they observe with contempt a passing troop of "the worst of the earth lovers," but then they notice with envy a pair of lovers in a pew below. Reversing their earlier judgment, The Third Priest confesses, speaking for them all:

> The lure of life! It has never lost its charm for me....
> The harmony!... How much greater is their reality than ours!
> And all because of their faith in it.[1]

In Wilder's play *And the Sea Shall Give Up Its Dead* the three characters, The Empress, Horatio Nissem, and Father Cosroe, are pictured as rising through the sea on Judgment Day. They are "slowly liberating [their] ... mind from the prides and prejudices and trivialities of a life-time,"[2] losing their particular characters, but the loss is painful. As each one realizes he will be reduced to his "quintessential matter," he cries out in anguish to retain his identity: "Let me keep my particular mind, O God, my own curious mind with all I have put into it."[3]

Wilder adapted to his play Dreiser's spirits with their nostalgia for material reality and their awareness at the same time of its limitations. The larger rhythm of both plays is the same, dramatizing a shift from scorn for what appear to be life's trivialities to a bittersweet appreciation of life by those who are no longer living. The religious tone of both plays is generalized, although Dreiser perhaps insists more heavily, through the Priests of Isis and the young lovers, on the identity of religion or life with love, a notion that Wilder developed elaborately in his novel *The Bridge of San Luis Rey*.

This same idea of forcing attention on life through a consideration of death was used to provide coherence and meaning to the episodic adventures of the hero in Wilder's first novel, *The Cabala,* which was published two years earlier than the Three Minute Plays though, of course, it had been written later. At the conclusion the hero is sailing to his native United States after a year in Italy, when suddenly the shade of Virgil manifests itself. Like the spirits in the plays, Virgil's shade cannot erase a longing for the world. He is caught between the

inexpressible beauty of Rome and the Mediterranean and the desira-
bility of Zion. *The Cabala* adds another dimension to the conflict,
since the hero is caught between European history and art, all of which
is alive in Rome but foreign to him, and his own identity as a new
man, an American. This was simply the novelization of a major struggle in Wilder's own writing career, and not until *Heaven's My Destination* — and the very title itself looks back to the conclusion of *The
Cabala* — did he enter safely into the gates of that Zion so desired by
Virgil and become a truly American writer.

Though Virgil's credentials as a guide for the soul are the very best,
Wilder's introduction of his ghost into what is essentially a realistic
novel reveals a problem of presentation that he had not yet solved and
which seriously flaws a remarkable book — more remarkable, even,
when one remembers that it is Wilder's first. In *The Woman of Andros* Wilder tried another answer, which, though it kept within the
bounds of more or less realistic storytelling, begs the question. Chrysis,
the Andrian, embodies the idea of living seen from the vantage point
of the dead in a myth or a parable. Wilder escaped the necessity to
keep to the limits set by the novel by having the very meaning of the
novel clarified not through his own story but through a story told by
one of his characters. To refute the idea that life in a family is not he-
roic, Chrysis tells the story of a young man who returns from the dead
for one day with the condition that he must be both "the participant
and the onlooker." He sees "that the living too are dead and that we
can only be said to be alive when our hearts are conscious of our treasure; for our hearts are not strong enough to love every moment."[4]

The Woman of Andros is the last time that Wilder was uncertain
in handling his material. Act III of *Our Town,* when Emily returns
from the dead for one day, is a version of the Andrian's myth in American dress, this time fully dramatized and integrated with the story.
Like the hero, Emily is compelled by her experience to bid a somewhat
reluctant but also relieved farewell to the living.

Certain places in the first complete manuscript of *Our Town* suggest that Wilder fretted over whether the audience would understand
what he had so carefully arranged. He tended to speak in his own
voice, rather than to dramatize what he knew. Near the end of the

third act is a short bit of dialogue deleted from the final version. The dead of Grover's Corners are sitting glumly waiting when Emily returns from her day in the past.

> EMILY: Mr. Stimson, did you go back?
>
> SIMON STIMSON (*harshly*): No. There was nothing I wanted to go back to.
>
> EMILY: Then you have forgotten it. You are ready for ... what comes next?
>
> SIMON STIMSON (*to the stage manager*): You tell her.
>
> STAGE MANAGER: Simon Stimson wants me to tell you that he is as much bound to the earth by hate as you may be bound to it by love.[5]

Here the Stage Manager, vastly oversimplifying, flatly and didactically states what Wilder later showed the audience: the idea that living itself without any sort of moral commitment to the difference between right and wrong, in this case love or hate, possesses the greatest value for man. In the final version Emily has just returned from her "day."

> SIMON STIMSON (*with mounting violence; bitingly*): Yes, now you know. Now you know! That's what it was to be alive. To move about in a cloud of ignorance; to go up and down trampling on the feelings of those ... of those about you. To spend and waste time as though you had a million years. To be always at the mercy of one self-centered passion, or another. Now you know — that's the happy existence you wanted to go back to. Ignorance and blindness.
>
> MRS. GIBBS: Simon Stimson, that ain't the whole truth and you know it.[6]

Simon Stimson's unkind words to Emily, especially with the powerful pause after "the feelings of those," coming directly after the painful experience of her twelfth birthday, present to the audience not only the very behavior his words condemn but also through his indignation his refusal to sink into indifference to a world that very possibly merits it. Simon Stimson's outburst, like the anger of a satirist, demonstrates a sharp awareness of unrealized, perhaps, but nonetheless genuine human possibilities in living. Just as Achilles in Book XI of the *Odyssey*, when he says that he would rather be a living slave than a dead king, commits himself to living rather than any idea or view of it, so Wilder in *Our Town* finally succeeded in dramatizing living — simple, daily living — rather than any conceptualized version of it.

In a letter to Mrs. George Pierce Baker, Wilder explained why he chose to portray living from the position of the dead, and at the same time he measured indirectly just how far he had developed from the Three Minute Plays and the influence of Dreiser.

> I had in mind especially the valley of the repentant Kings in about the 8th Canto of the Purgatorio. Same patience, waiting; same muted pain; same oblique side-glances back to earth. Dante has an angel descend mightily and after slaying a serpent who tries to the [*sic*] enter the Valley every evening, stands guard the rest of the night. Most commentators agree that the allegory means: from now on the Dead must be guarded from memories of their earthly existence and from irruptions of the old human nature associations.[7]

Wilder means by "human nature" something like identity with time and place. It is not unfeeling of Emily when she says to Mrs. Gibbs of George's mourning: "They don't understand, do they?,"[8] or as in the typescript of the first full version: "They don't listen to what they're [*sic*] heart tells them."[9] Emily is simply saying that the living do not understand the dead, who are removed from the obfuscating details of life, and that the living should continue to do their very best with life while they still have it. The dead appreciate life painfully well; fortunately they are forgetting.

In the Andrian's story the hero is required to return "with a mind divided into two persons, — the participant and the onlooker." Emily also returns with a mind divided. The Stage Manager says, "You not only live it; but you watch yourself living it."[10] Emily participates, and Emily also feels the anguish of her own and her family's inadequacy to life. This double vision acquires additional strength from having the audience witness it. It is more moving to watch Emily than it could possibly be to hear Chrysis tell about the hero, for Chrysis' story remains abstract and distant, whereas Emily's plight is arranged not only so that it happens before our eyes but also so that it might be that of each one of us.

The Janus-headed observation of the human animal, one face gazing at the living and the other at the dead, pops up in various disguises throughout Wilder's work. In *Heaven's My Destination* the hero, George Brush, who is in spirit, at least, an autobiographical character, meets during one of his picaresque adventures a movie director. George Burkin, the director, whose name suggests a closer relationship with Brush than he himself recognizes, has been arrested as a peeping Tom. He explains with some impatience to Brush that when he looks, an unobserved outsider, through windows at people at their daily tasks, he sees their very souls. The false movements people make when they function socially fall away to expose the barest rhythm of living. Wilder is himself a kind of Burkin; he has looked closely through people's windows and then used what he observed to make his plays and novels. Burkin says, "I'm the greatest artist America ever had in any line."[11] He and Wilder both are captured by the special feeling Americans have about their living: that it is truer without manners and codified social patterns.

At the conclusion of *Heaven's My Destination,* Brush cannot answer No to his own question, "Isn't the principle of a thing more important than the people that live under the principle?"[12] When he cannot force his life and the life of others to fit any hard and fast plan, he collapses physically and is without any desire to recover his life. He is on the way to taking the advice of Job's wife to curse God and die when a package arrives for him, containing a spoon. It comes from a Catholic priest, Father Pasziewski, whom Brush has never met but who has thought a great deal about Brush. Father Pasziewski has known he was dying and wishes to be remembered; he thinks that Brush may use the spoon in some way. This gift of the homely spoon from beyond the grave triggers in Brush the desire to live again.

Looking through windows and a gift from the dead combine to make still another variation in *Sloth,* a one-act play from a series *The Seven Deadly Sins* on which Wilder is presently working. The play, moreover, has an immediate connection with Chrysis' story in *The Woman of Andros*. Wilder has said that Pamphilus in the novel illustrated in part the medieval sin acedia, or sloth,[13] which, more than idleness or laziness, is a totally enervating despair. In the manuscript of the first version of *The Woman of Andros* one of the themes is noted as "To die to oneself,"[14] and this failure to live with all one's energy, like Brush's sickness, is the meaning of sloth.

The play is about a Mr. Hawkins, who has claimed that life looks as though it were seen through a window; it can be viewed, but it is separate and silent. He is bequeathed twenty thousand dollars by an old woman who had once told him, "Why don't you do it? . . . Really stand outside and look through some windows."[15] It is peculiarly American that it is money that provides Hawkins' opportunity and also peculiar to Wilder's vision that, like Emily and the hero of the Andrian's tale and Pasziewski's spoon, it is provoked from beyond the grave. The result is that he decides to watch his wife and daughter through a window and then to commit suicide. What he sees through the window—his wife and daughter sewing—brings about a great change in his life. He tells his wife, "I've decided to move to 'here.' To take up residence as they say. I'll move in tonight."[16] Hawkins has seen what it really is to be outside the window and at the same time what a great treasure it is to be inside. Like Emily, he understands that life at its simplest has a value too great to measure. Unlike Emily, he can walk through the door and rejoin life.

But Wilder has not forgotten that daily living is too dear to be realized consciously or completely. Mrs. Hawkins complains to her husband that he is not supposed to see her except from within himself, in an almost instinctive loving. Our public attitude and face are like an incognito we put on paradoxically in order to be recognized by the world.

Wilder also adapted his idea to laughter. *The Merchant of Yonkers* is a farce-comedy about the adventure of living. It opened the same year as *Our Town,* but did not achieve any success until Wilder modified it a bit, changing the name to *The Matchmaker,* for the Edinburgh Festival of 1954. As Barnaby explains at its conclusion, the play is about adventure: "We hope you have just the right amount of sitting quietly at home and just the right amount of . . . adventure."[17]

Earlier than *The Merchant of Yonkers,* in the one-act play *Such Things Only Happen in Books* from *The Long Christmas Dinner,* Wilder experimented with the relationship between sitting quietly at home and adventure. In that play a novelist with his wife has taken an old New England house. He is having trouble writing a new book because all plot situations seem to him impossibly false. The play shows the audience — although the novelist never learns — that his wife has a lover, his maid's brother is an escaped convict, and the former owner of the house was murdered by his children, who have returned secretly to the scene of their crime. The novelist gloomily plays solitaire through most of the play — very badly, because he refuses to look under the cards. His wife slyly suggests that he may not see all the moves. The play is a simple and good-humored joke; none of the situations is distasteful. And although the audience are not expected to *believe* the play — it is a fiction, after all, as the title warns — life is portrayed as an adventure at least as good as fiction if we take the wife's advice and pay close attention so as not to miss any of the moves.

The great achievement of *The Merchant of Yonkers,* Mrs. Dolly Levi, has a more successful imagination than the novelist of *Such Things Only Happen in Books.* Her individuality, her vitality, and her imagination soar beyond the simple plot of the play. She, like Wilder himself, is able at will to call to life and endow with personality the other characters of the play. She forces them as well as the audience to seize life. As she dashes on and off the stage, not only does she arrange the plot and the lives of the characters but she also lifts both from the level of an uninteresting generalization.

Cornelius Hackl, chief clerk of the merchant, Vandergelder, is a timid and dull man who has worked his entire life for security. His overpowering but secret desire is to be once in his life really alive, to have an adventure, and he takes the first step when he goes to New York. Almost by accident he finds himself hiding in Mrs. Molloy's cabinet. Mrs. Levi, who knows he is there, creates for him on the spot a new and dashing character, primarily, it is true, to fool Vandergelder and Mrs. Molloy. Mrs. Levi has really been campaigning for her own marriage to Vandergelder. The final result, however, is that Cornelius marries Mrs. Molloy. He has his adventure; it is one of the heart.

Mrs. Levi has generated the force that demands that Cornelius and Mrs. Molloy realize their potential selves, although they are little more than stock theatrical characters. She has compelled them, just for one evening, to assume the individuality that she has provided and briefly become adequate for living.

The Merchant of Yonkers complements *Our Town* as the mask of comedy does that of tragedy, although *Our Town* is not a tragedy in spite of its potentially tragic vision. Emily learns that life is "too wonderful for anybody to realize" it, but the Stage Manager tells her that the "saints and poets, maybe . . . do some";[18] that is, they have some hint of the wonder of life. This is not emphasized very strongly in *Our Town,* but it is an important part of the meaning of *The Merchant of Yonkers,* for Dolly Levi, like Burkin in *Heaven's My Destination,* is a poet. She says of herself to Kemper, a painter:

> Nature is never completely satisfactory and must be corrected. Well, I'm like you artists. Life as it is, is never quite interesting enough for me, . . . I'm bored . . . with life as it is, and so I do things. I put my hand in here, and I put my hand in there, and I watch and I listen, — and I am often very much amused.[19]

Dolly Levi knows the wonder of life, and she knows, too, that it takes only a little prodding for the wonder to reveal itself. She knows also, however, how easy it is not to be alive. In the revised version, *The Matchmaker,* she says:

> After my husband's death I retired into myself. . . . I was a perfectly contented woman. And one night, after two years of this, an oak leaf fell out of my Bible. I had placed it there on the day my husband asked me to marry him; a perfectly good oak leaf — but without color and without life. And suddenly I realized that for a long time I had not shed one tear; nor had I been filled with the wonderful hope that something or other would turn out well. I saw that I was like that oak leaf, and on that night I decided to rejoin the human race.[20]

She is concerned, of course, only with what is usually regarded as ordinary in life: living itself. What she arranges is banal, really — marriages. But it is marriage that brings two people together, brings them to life.

Mrs. Levi, through marriage, saves Vandergelder from his money; she persuades him of the necessity to spend it. More importantly, she has rescued him from the stock character of the miser. As she herself suggests, she is returning him to the human race.

All the characters have been "saved" by Mrs. Levi, but they are worth saving. Vandergelder, beneath his miserly exterior, is a human being. In his soliloquy in the first act he confides to the audience a desire to release his humanity, although he perhaps does not fully understand the consequences of his longing.

> There's nothing like mixing with women to bring out all the foolishness in a man of sense, but it's a risk I'm willing to take.
>
> I've just turned sixty; I've just laid side by side the last dollar of my first . . . half million. Even if I should lose my head a little I have enough money to put it back. After fifty years' caution and hard work I've a right to a little risk and adventure and I'm thinking of getting married. Yes, like all you other fools, I'm ready to risk a little security for a certain amount of adventure.[21]

According to him, fools are distinguished from sensible men by their attitude toward money. Vandergelder tells the world that almost all men are fools and that he is one of the few men of sense put here to keep watch over all these fools. He confesses, however, that he is willing to risk foolishness himself, to risk some of his money for adventure. But he does not stop being a miser, for he says also that he is considering marriage because he likes his "house run with order, comfort, and economy. That's a woman's work ."[22]

Precisely what Mrs. Levi accomplishes with Vandergelder she describes in her soliloquy in the fourth act. She agrees with Vandergelder that all people are fools, but, she says, "there comes a moment in everybody's life when he must decide whether he'll live among them or not, really live among human beings or not, — a fool among fools, or a fool alone."[23] She describes the person who has refused the human race as one, like George Brush, "who makes plans to improve and restrict the human race according to patterns of his own."[24] Mrs. Levi rescues the other characters of the play from such a "blue-print world." In terms of the plot, she has pulled them back into accepting the human race; in terms of the style of the play, she has saved them from being merely empty characters in a farce — miser, young fool, widow.

Wilder hopes that in demonstrating to the characters of the play how very precious and difficult being alive is, he has also shown it to the audience. The meaning is the same as that of *Our Town;* the manner of presentation is different. Whether the audience weep over Emily or laugh with Mrs. Levi is really of little importance when the plays are done and the curtain is down. The danger to Wilder's vision is the audience itself, the possibility that they will regard Emily's plight sentimentally so that it becomes meaningless and that they will see only the comedy and nothing more in *The Merchant of Yonkers.*

When *The Merchant of Yonkers* was published in 1939, it carried an interesting and troublesome note on the copyright page: "This play is based upon a comedy by Johann Nestroy, *Einen Jux will er sich Machen* (*sic: machen*) (Vienna, 1842) which was in turn based upon an English original, *A Well Spent Day* (*sic: A Day Well Spent*) (London, 1835), by John Oxenford."[25]

A Day Well Spent is a one-act play in nine scenes that has no merit whatever. The dialogue is pompous, the characters are lifeless, and the humor is without imagination. Its single virtue is that its plot with no essential changes was used by Nestroy for his play. *Einen Jux,* on the other hand, is a full four-act play that abounds with comic vitality. Nestroy has followed Oxenford's plotting, but has embellished it with social comment, songs, expanded dialogue, and one additional character. But in spite of the clever songs and satiric examination of society, it holds the stage today more because of its fantastic flights of the Viennese argot than for any other reason. Wilder transformed Nestroy's satirical-comic play into a farce, making no effort to reproduce reality; his interest lay rather in frankly imitating it. However, through ignorance, the reviewers and the public also therefore assumed that Nestroy's play was likewise a farce and that Wilder had merely adapted or translated the original, and none too well. The production was not liked; the play was not a success.

Much of the play's difficulty was certainly the fault of its director, Max Reinhardt, and his failure to understand its special American qualities. He had a well-deserved reputation in Europe. Although his productions of *The Miracle* and *A Midsummer Night's Dream* had achieved a certain success in America, while in exile here he languished in California far from Broadway. Wilder wrote *The Merchant of Yonkers* especially for him, and the play was supposed to bring him to New York. It was a strategic error.

Reinhardt was expert at directing Nestroy's kind of play for German audiences, but he seemed to understand neither Wilder's play nor the American crowd. His reputation depended on his creating style through elaborate stage effects and slow pace. His strength was a self-conscious attitude toward historical time in terms of conventions, costumes, and scenery, but this style had a serious weakness: a tendency to disperse the meaning of the play through too great a concentration on unimportant detail. Wilder's play is not a period piece. To emphasize its time and place through visual effects is to destroy its immediacy, which is established in part by the deliberate removal of all marks of any particular traditional culture. Whatever was in the play that belonged to the box-set stage was there to be laughed at in order to destroy it, not to be revived with the idea of recreating the atmosphere from which it emerged. The machinery of farce restored the play from a limited and vague comedy and emphasized the clear vision of repeated existing through the use of convention and type characters.

Still Reinhardt was a great artist, and although Wilder's vision probably would not have survived under Reinhardt's hand, the play might have been a success if the central role of Dolly Levi, which does not appear in either Oxenford's or Nestroy's play, had been successfully cast. As a result of circumstances that had nothing to do with her ability, an actress was selected who was a disaster. She would not learn her lines except during rehearsal, and she frequently missed rehearsals. She resisted direction. In every sense she was unsuitable for the part.

Reinhardt apparently concentrated his efforts on the other actors, who were excellent and responsive. The play grew unbalanced as comic stage business mushroomed until it lost even all pretense of developing from the action. The meaning of the play disappeared under the elaborate and carefully staged but static picture effects. Though the curtain falls in most American theaters by eleven o'clock, musicals sometimes excepted, *The Merchant of Yonkers* ran at first almost until midnight. The great director was handicapped by his star and his own sensitiveness. When he was approached with suggestions, his despair over doing anything with the central role, combined with his pleasure and delight in what was happening with the other actors, made him deaf. Day after day during rehearsal Wilder, his sister Isabel, the producer, everybody, watched with amazed horror as Wilder's American farce grew into a middle-European comedy. Despite frantic efforts to doctor the play, it flopped, and not until its recent revival under a new name with Ruth Gordon playing an exceptionally fine Dolly Levi and its even more recent musical version has it had the success it deserves, though like so much success, perhaps for the wrong reasons. With generous recognition of his theatrical genius and friendship and with a freedom from rancor rare in the theater, Wilder dedicated the new version, *The Matchmaker,* to Reinhardt also.

In *Our Town* and *The Merchant of Yonkers* the focus on life is individual. Four years later in *The Skin of Our Teeth* the awareness expanded to mankind considered as a single group. "*Our Town,*" Wilder said, "is the life of the family seen from a telescope five miles away. *The Skin of Our Teeth* is the destiny of the whole human group seen from a telescope 1,000 miles away."[26] The individual and the family were retained in the Antrobus family cluster, but the family, along with Sabina, the maid, were representative of the entire human race and its progress through time. Wilder wrote to Edward Sheldon (an extraordinary man who was, though blind and crippled, to many people, including Wilder, a seemingly infinite source of cheer, encouragement, and good sense; to whom *The Ides of March* is dedicated; and who was the inspiration for the character Lucius Mamilius Turrinus in that book) that the play held "all the implications that were real to me: man's spiral progress and his progression through trial and error."[27]

Perhaps nowhere is the repeated danger of the racial despair in living dramatized more clearly than at the play's conclusion. The world has all but been destroyed through war, and Antrobus, returning home, has lost the "most important thing of all: The desire to begin again, to start building."[28] He is interrupted by Sabina, who asks permission to go to the movies, where "they're giving away a hand-painted soup-tureen to every lady."[29] She has illegally in her possession some beef cubes for her admission. When Mrs. Antrobus explains that she should turn them in to the Center downtown, Sabina cries, "I didn't make this war. I didn't ask for it. And in my opinion, after anybody's gone through what we've gone through, they have a right to grab what they can find."[30]

Sabina's foolish, perfectly ordinary human behavior, neither good nor very bad, and above all her obvious need for help in her moral and emotional muddle are Antrobus' inspiration. Wilder has not falsified his situation by sentimentally suggesting that human beings are good and therefore deserve life. Sabina's first impulse was selfish; she wanted the beef cubes for her own use. He has, however, through a series of incongruous juxtapositioning of desires and needs, established a wide range and variety of life. The free soup tureen acknowledges man's inane acquisitiveness. But, like George Brush's spoon, a soup tureen is useful. Sabina wants it presumably to put soup in; she has an almost unconscious desire to return to the normal. The soup tureen with its hand-painted decorations and its false elegance pitifully puts the idea of nourishment above the level of mere animal survival. Furthermore, in its connection with the movies, it establishes dramatic representation at the very beginning of life. Sabina's desire to go to the movies is idiotic; but her desire for escape, pleasure, and, who knows, a glimmer of the vision that only the theater can convey are to the point.

Wilder throughout his work has struggled against the belief that human beings are bad and must be improved in living. Antrobus wants merely to help people be themselves. He is all the leaders of mankind who could not prevent themselves from writing, inventing, or legislating, and he is urged forward first of all by the love he has for his family. The family, all mankind, does not particularly deserve his love or his work, but the family is based on the promise and can function only out of that promise which is at the beginning of life. Mrs. Antrobus, in the second act when Antrobus seems about to desert her for Sabina, explains the strength and consequences of marriage.

> I didn't marry you because you were perfect. I didn't even marry you because I loved you. I married you because you gave me a promise. . . . That promise made up for your faults. And the promise I gave you

made up for mine. . . . And when our children were growing up, it wasn't a house that protected them; and it wasn't our love, that protected them — it was that promise.

And when that promise is broken — this can happen![31]

She removes the raincoat that their daughter is wearing to reveal her dressed in scarlet stockings, which ironically represent the disintegration of their hope.

And in the second act when Mrs. Antrobus addresses the convention of man, reciting the history of marriage, she concludes:

> My husband says that the watchword for the year is Enjoy Yourselves. I think that's very open to misunderstanding. My watchword for the year is: Save the Family. It's held together for over five thousand years: Save it![32]

Mrs. Antrobus knows that the Sabinas do not last very long, because while they are fun, they are not essential to life. Explaining more straightforwardly his ideas, Wilder told the *Paris Review* interviewer:

> Love started out as a concomitant of reproduction; it is what makes new life and then shelters it. It is therefore an affirmation about existence and belief in value. Tens of thousands of years have gone by; more complicated forms of society and of consciousness have arisen. Love acquired a wide variety of secondary expressions. It got mixed up with a power conflict between male and female; it got cut off from its primary intentions and took its place among the refinements of psychic life, and in the cult of pleasure; it expanded beyond the relations of the couple and family and reappeared as philanthropy; it attached itself to man's ideas about the order of the universe and was attributed to the gods and God.[33]

Wilder here clarifies the conflict between Antrobus and his wife and expands the watchword "Enjoy Yourself." Like Mrs. Antrobus, he returns to the promise that underlies love.

> I always see beneath it, nevertheless, the urge that strives toward justifying life, harmonizing it — the source of energy on which life must draw in order to better itself. . . . This attitude has so much the character of self-evidence for me that I am unable to weigh or even "hear" any objections to it.[34]

Antrobus is significantly different from Emily. He refuses to join the dead and their gradual forgetting. He desires strongly to remember, actively to be alive, and constructively to move ahead. "All I ask," he says, "is the chance to build new worlds."[35] He is the embodiment of American optimism as he willfully ignores any inadequacies in himself or in his situation. The simple possession of life is regarded as being as much a duty as a privilege. Antrobus' witnessing Sabina's giving up of the beef cubes confused with her pathetic need to escape to the movies is similar to Emily's reviewing her birthday. Emily's gifts from her parents and George are both too wonderful and so pitiful in the perspective of a life already lived. Emily returns to the dead because to be with the living is unbearable for her. Antrobus, as the audience of *Our Town* should do, assumes with renewed vigor the duty of living.

Wilder ignores a coherent view of the peculiar details of life. He invests living with value by forcing the attention of his characters and thus of his audience on the horror of its absence. The hero is the person who is most aware of his living. He can be recognized by his ability to love, for to love is to be vulnerable. The vulnerability dramatizes everything that might be lost, but at the same time how much is possible in present living. Love, however, is only a sign of living. The ultimate meaning of living for Wilder, as suggested by Father Pasziewski and the Bible from which Mrs. Levi's leaf falls, is religious.

II

THE RELIGIOUS LIFE

---

*By tacit assumption ... the religious life is
one of the few absolute human values.*

"ALMOST all of the plays in this book are religious, but religious in
that dilute fashion that is a believer's concession to a contemporary
standard of good manners.... It is the kind of work that I would most
like to do well, in spite of the fact that there has seldom been an age in
literature when such a vein was less welcome and less understood."[1]
In this uneasy, almost apologetic way Wilder introduced his first plays
in *The Angel That Troubled the Waters*. All the Three Minute Plays
in this volume are religious, though some, like *Leviathan,* conceding
to contemporary good manners, could be considered such only
through interpretation. Others, however, like the title play, which was
suggested by John 5:4 — "For an angel went down at a certain season
into the pool, and troubled the water" — are fundamentally religious.
They are in the exegetical tradition of the Protestant sermon which
takes a biblical text and then expounds upon it, examining some of its
implications for the Christian life. This is the kind of play Wilder once
said he "would most like to do well."

Thornton Wilder's interest in religion is not hard to explain. His
family and home were devoutly Protestant; his parents were actively
involved in church education; his brother Amos, who has himself
written some volumes of religious poetry, went on to become a teacher
of theology at Harvard. While in China, Wilder attended a mission
school, at least for a while. His father, thinking perhaps that his own
alma mater, Yale, was too worldly for Thornton, chose Oberlin for his

first two college years, and Oberlin was then emphatically religious in its undergraduate life and curriculum. Escape for the writer from such an environment was neither easy nor quick. Only much later, under the influence of Gertrude Stein and her writing and Sören Kierkegaard's philosophy, did Wilder depart from the limited devout Protestant sermonizing of his early training to explore a more intellectual and a more generalized expression of religion. In 1928, the date of the introduction to the Three Minute Plays, he still wrote unaffectedly of the "believer," presumably himself.

The Trumpet Shall Sound, Wilder's first long play, was written along with most of the Three Minute Plays, and like them it is a kind of sermon. It has been published only in the *Yale Literary Magazine* one act at a time in four consecutive issues, and in 1926 Richard Boleslavsky produced it for the American Laboratory Theatre in New York. Its text is from I Corinthians 15:52 — "for the trumpet shall sound, and the dead shall be raised incorruptible, and we shall be changed." It is about judgment. In terms of the plot the judgment is by a householder, Peter Magnus, perhaps a kind of ironic modern St. Peter, who returns suddenly, after having been away for a long time, to consider the trust of his servants. Actually the events of the plot are a thin disguise for the real business of the play, which is an examination of divine justice and mercy and of Christian rebirth.

The story is of a young girl, Flora, who gains control of Magnus' house through the death of the butler. Secretly, in order to make money for her lover, she rents rooms to all who are cast out from society. The reference to "the halt, the deaf, the dumb and the blind" in Wilder's description of these roomers is surely to Luke 14. A man had said to Jesus, "Blessed is he that shall eat bread in the kingdom of God." Jesus reproached him with a parable in which a man whose friends have refused to eat with him sends his servant to go into the streets of the city. He is told, "Bring in hither the poor, and the maimed, and the halt, and the blind." An oblique reference is also implied to John 5:3, the verse immediately preceding the one that provided the title to *The Angel That Troubled the Waters* — there "lay a great multitude of impotent folk, of blind, halt, withered, waiting for the moving of the water." The Bible texts, though they are only in stage directions, clearly suggest that the people who take the rooms should, because of their afflictions, be more welcome to man's home and heart than those who have no need. To succor them is truly to "eat bread in the kingdom of God."

The furnace in the house produces no heat, although it frequently smokes through the heat registers, filling the rooms. The cold combined with the smoke calls to mind hell in Milton's *Paradise Lost*. It is as though the characters were waiting, each in his hell, for Jesus to defeat sin and death, precisely what is to happen when the trumpet of the title sounds. Significantly the repair of the furnace is promised for midnight, the time that Magnus arranges for his judgment.

With a blast from a conch shell and the command *fiat Justitia,* Magnus disposes of the roomers. He forgives the intrusion into his house, but he cannot, he says, absolve "the thievers, the fraudulent, the blasphemers, and the filthy."[2] One of the best-developed of Wilder's roomers is Dabney, who earlier in life was a ship's captain who deserted when his ship sank, permitting all aboard to go to the bottom with it. Ironically, he had been converted from the life of a sailor to one devoted to the salvation of souls; the fatal crossing was to have been his last before he launched himself in his new calling. When the trumpet sounds and the dead are raised to confront him, it will be a chilly meeting. As Dabney leaves with Magnus' absolution, he asks for mercy for Flora, whose behavior he explains self-righteously as the result of self-seeking and a weak or nonexistent conscience!

One by one, the roomers shift their blame to Flora and are sent on their way guiltless by Magnus. Carlo, Flora's lover for whom she has acted, especially is welcomed back from her "ambitious, unscrupulous and uncontrolled" clutches. As it turns out, Flora alone is sufficiently guilty to be punished. Accepting the burden of guilt and betrayed by all, with Carlo's single gift, a small pistol, she shoots herself. As a final irony, Miss Flecker, Magnus' informer, is rewarded with the position of housekeeper. Although she piously protests that she had expected nothing in return for her earlier watchfulness, the audience know this to be a lie.

The irony of the total failure of human justice, emphasized by Magnus' name and its suggestion of greatness and generosity, is obvious enough. Human justice succeeds only when the impulses of mercy and love are permitted their rightful place. Magnus has, in the tradition of the man of hybris, forgotten his own humanity in his attempt to play god. But the play has another meaning perhaps equally obvious. Justice has indeed been done. Magnus' judgment dramatizes the frightening warning of Jesus: "Judge not, that ye be not judged." Each of the characters has been both Judge and Judged: as each of them betrays Flora in his own way, he exposes and condemns himself.

But Flora's suicide seems merely melodramatic. The eventual triumph of divine justice after the curtain falls is not truly part of the play. Magnus grudgingly admits a justice beyond his, a wiser one where it is possible that his verdicts, some of them, *may* be reversed, but the religious values which ought to give Flora's death meaning are only indirectly expressed: through biblical reference as in the title and stage directions, through literary allusion as with the Miltonic setting, and through mysterious information, such as that a room in the stable had been rented to a man and woman because the house was full, which, no doubt, is to convey the hope of the stable in Bethlehem. Only much later as in *The Skin of Our Teeth* could Wilder actually transform such material into the very action and texture of his play.

Wilder's next two novels, *The Bridge of San Luis Rey* and *The Woman of Andros*, though they are not unqualifiedly successful, achieve a more skillful solution to the problem of representing the mystery of divine justice. In the manuscript of the first version of *The Woman of Andros* two themes of the novel are noted: "The gods have a great gift for those who love them: they turn even their weaknesses and their mistakes to gold," and "What we love in another person is an hint of immortality."[3] As the first chapter of this book demonstrates in part, Wilder has remained remarkably faithful to his metaphysic, artless though it may be, clarifying it and bringing it to a fullness through a developing aesthetic. Both these themes noted constitute a major part of the meaning of *The Trumpet Shall Sound*, and they form the substance of *The Bridge of San Luis Rey* also. Further, they are found in *Heaven's My Destination* and *Our Town*, his first fully successful novel and play, as well as in all his work to follow.

Brother Juniper, in *The Bridge of San Luis Rey*, having never learned or perhaps having forgotten the lesson so painfully acquired by Job, tries to "justify the ways of God to man" by rational inquiry and analysis. Like any good social scientist, he has laboratory control, the collapse of the bridge, "a sheer act of God." Brother Juniper's efforts to place theology among the exact sciences leads directly to confusion, the Inquisition, and the fire, where calling "upon St. Francis and leaning upon a flame he smiled and died." But Juniper's inquiry and its conclusion are not meaningless, for among the witnesses to his burning "were many who believed . . . that his intention, at least, had been for faith . . . for he was much loved."[4]

The Marquesa de Montemayor, to consider only one of the five people who fell with the bridge, let her life be ruled by a single passion, her love for her daughter, though "not for her daughter's sake but for her own." Since the daughter is four thousand miles away in Spain, the Marquesa's consuming activity is, like Mme. de Sévigné's on which hers is patterned, writing brilliant letters to provoke her daughter's admiration. Everything in the life around her is either material for the letters or disregarded. One day by chance she reads a letter written by her young companion to the Mother Superior of the convent where the young girl was raised and educated. The letter is written with such love that the Marquesa is filled with envy for the person to whom it is addressed. Pepita, her companion, astonishes her by telling her that the letter will never be sent because it is not brave. Understanding as if for the first time that "she had never brought courage to either life or love,"[5] she promises herself to begin a new life, and, sitting down, she writes what she calls her first letter, free from the tyranny of her demanding love. Two days later she falls with the bridge.

But the fall of the bridge is not disconnected in time, and the Marquesa's discovery is not empty. Among "the events that would not have been the same without the fall of the bridge," Wilder describes a meeting between the Marquesa's daughter and Pepita's Mother Superior. Both are changed by the Marquesa's last letter: the daughter recognizes her mother's love, and the Mother Superior is relieved of the despair over what she considered the meaninglessness of her life. The novel then ends with the famous last sentence: "There is a land of

the living and a land of the dead and the bridge is love, the only survival, the only meaning."[6] God does indeed work in mysterious ways,
hidden from the simple faith of Brother Juniper but not foreign to it.

The literal bridge has become a metaphor, and the reader is left
with that "hint of immortality" Wilder described as one of the themes
of *The Woman of Andros*. The weakness of the Marquesa, her tyran-
nical love, resulted in her golden letters and furthermore in the recognition of life by her daughter and the Mother Superior. One is almost
tempted to pronounce patly like a Sunday School teacher, "God is
love."

The Bridge of San Luis Rey was an astounding success. It found
300,000 and more readers in America and was translated into many
foreign languages. A "philosophical novel" (which *The Bridge of San
Luis Rey* is not) amazed the critics by becoming a best seller. It won
a Pulitzer Prize. It was sold to the movies. And it built for Mr. Wilder
and his family an attractive and charming house just outside New
Haven, Connecticut. Almost four decades later, however, critical judgment has many reservations about it. Perhaps the doubts over the use
of past time, the eighteenth century, and the foreign place, Peru,
where Wilder had not been at the time he wrote the novel, can be dismissed as either irrelevant or significant in that, as deliberately willed
by the imagination, they suggest timelessness and a detachment from
a particular place. Though much has been made of Wilder's sources
for the novel — Prosper Mérimée and Mme. de Sévigné, among others
— this is unimportant. Wilder's use of Roman Catholicism, rather
than his own native Protestantism, however, exposes a weakness in the
book. Catholicism is presented as mere aesthetic, that is, as color,
movement, music, and other outward forms; the meaning and life of
the novel's characters is closer to old-fashioned Protestant individual
will. Much more important, the rhetoric used to convey the meaning
of the novel at most critical points is in the worst sense literary and,
like the Catholicism, false. The conclusion to "Part One: Perhaps an
Accident" reads: "Some say that we shall never know and that to the
gods we are like flies that the boys kill on a summer day, and some say,
on the contrary, that the very sparrows do not lose a feather that has
not been brushed away by the finger of God."[7] This limpid and exqui-

site rendering certainly of Shakespeare (*King Lear*) in the first part and probably of Shakespeare (*Hamlet*) in the second part seems trivial and merely pretty when the original is recalled. Worse, the feeling behind the words is suspect because it has not been recreated for the novel, but appears a graceful decoration like sugar roses on a cake, lovely but not very good to eat.

Chrysis, the Andrian in *The Woman of Andros,* like Flora and the Mother Superior, provides a home for the outcast and infirm. And like Emily in *Our Town* and Alcestis, whom she in fact mentions, and the survivors of the bridge, she returns from being a dead one in despair to a new appreciation of life. Her return, though of short duration and incompletely understood, is brought about through her awakened love for Pamphilus, the hero of the novel. Her gift for him, like the Marquesa's letter and Emily's birthday, is a reawakening in him of praise for "all living, the bright and the dark," and once again Wilder has demonstrated that "hint of immortality." In this novel, Wilder deliberately chose a pre-Christian era, though the beginning and the conclusion enclose it in the birth of Jesus. This Christmas envelope is more successful than the offstage Holy Family in *The Trumpet Shall Sound* and the Roman Catholicism of *The Bridge of San Luis Rey,* but the nagging question remains: Why was it necessary at all? Apparently Wilder still did not trust his skill in narration; perhaps his distrust was justified. Malcolm Cowley, in his introduction to the reprint collection of the three novels, wrote, "Because of its historical theme, I suspect that the book did not engage his deepest feelings, and it ends rather hastily, with the heroine and her child killed off in a sentence."[8] Aside from the facts that Glycerium, the girl who is "killed off," is not the heroine, that one sentence is as good as a page or more, and that the novel is not a historical one, Cowley feels the same vague disappointment that almost every reader of *The Woman of Andros* is aware of. The symptoms are common in Wilder's early work: the melodramatic suicide of Flora, the preachy, somewhat inflated concluding sentence to *The Bridge of San Luis Rey*. Wilder, I feel, simply did not know how to stop his story, and only after he learned carefully some of Gertrude Stein's lessons was he successful in concluding; but more of this in the chapter on Narration.

The Woman of Andros was as gossiped-about a flop as *The Bridge of San Luis Rey* had been a success. Michael Gold chose its publication to write a retrospective review of Wilder's novels in the *New Republic,* shrilly and angrily scolding him for not hewing to the Marxist line.

> And is this the style with which to express America? Is this the speech of a pioneer continent? . . . Where are the modern streets of New York, Chicago and New Orleans in these little novels? Where are the cotton mills, and the murder of Ella May and her songs? Where are the child slaves of the beet fields? . . .
>
> This genteel spirit of the new parlor-Christianity pervades every phrase of Mr. Wilder's rhetoric. What gentle theatrical sighs! what lovely, well composed deaths and martyrdoms! What languishings and flutterings of God's sinning doves![9]

If Gold and his beet fields seem creaky and comic today, they did not in 1930. The writers and critics of social injustice had the day, and it was not a short one. The result was an unofficial hands-off attitude by critics. Wilder was somehow not respectable, and he could be insulted in a public place, for example, with some approbation. Mary McCarthy sums it up with her usual forthrightness when she recalls: "How uneasy I felt when I decided that I *liked* Thornton Wilder's *Our Town.* Could this mean that there was something the matter with me? Was I starting to sell out? Such haunting fears, like the fear of impotence in men, were common in the avant-garde in those days."[10] *The Woman of Andros* is a special mark on the page of Wilder's history for several reasons. It brought the first of several scandalous critical attacks on his work that were more obfuscating than clarifying, and it marks the close of his early work.

The one-act plays of *The Long Christmas Dinner* are a kind of transition from Wilder's early religious views to the more interesting methods of expression of them in his mature work. The action of one of the plays, *Pullman Car Hiawatha,* is to locate the car in terms first of its inhabitants, then geographically as it moves across the country, meteorologically, astronomically, and finally and most importantly, theologically — in the mind of God. The location of its position, managed by short speeches from the inhabitants of the car and from actors who represent the town, the field, the ghost of a dead workman, the

hours, the planets, and two archangels, is, of course, similar to the conclusion to *The Skin of Our Teeth* and the speeches of the Hours, nine
o'clock through midnight. Each repeats a few words of a philosopher:
Spinoza:

> After experience had taught me that the common occurrences of daily
> life are vain and futile; and I saw that all the objects of my desire and
> fear were in themselves nothing good nor bad save insofar as the mind
> was affected by them; I at length determined to search out whether
> there was something truly good and communicable to man.

Without a pause the words from Plato follow:

> Then tell me, O Critias, how will a man choose the ruler that shall rule
> over him? Will he not choose a man who has first established order in
> himself, knowing that any decision that has its spring from anger or
> pride or vanity can be multiplied a thousand-fold in its effects upon the
> citizens?

Then Aristotle:

> This good estate of the mind possessing its object in energy we call di-
> vine. This we mortals have occasionally and it is this energy which is
> pleasantest and best. But God has it always. It is wonderful in us; but
> in Him how much more wonderful.

Finally the unknown writer of Genesis:

> In the beginning, God created the Heavens and the Earth; and the
> Earth was waste and void; and the darkness was upon the face of the
> deep. And the Lord said let there be light and there was light.[11]

Selected and arranged for a cumulative effect, these speeches suggest in a general way the meaning in life. Life has whatever meaning
the mind chooses to give it, as in Spinoza. Further, each man must
give his own life significance by discipline, as in Plato. The discipline
participates somehow as a small part of a force greater than man
which is God, as in Aristotle. And finally, God is the beginning and
end of all things, as the opening of the Bible repeats.

The idea of ultimate location of all the petty, everyday actions of
everybody in the mind of God is illustrated also in the first act of *Our
Town,* when Rebecca tells George of a letter Jane Crofut received ad-

dressed "Jane Crofut; The Crofut Farm; Grover's Corners; Sutton County; New Hampshire; United States of America; . . . Continent of North America; Western Hemisphere; the Earth; the Solar System; the Universe; the Mind of God."[12] The passage, similar to one in James Joyce's *A Portrait of the Artist as a Young Man,* sums up the first act of *Our Town,* hinting at a meaning that is religious in feeling without depending on biblical text or dogma of any special faith or sect.

The change in Wilder's understanding of religion undeniably was aided and clarified by his friendship with Gertrude Stein and his reading of her work. Wilder first met Gertrude Stein in the winter of 1935 in Chicago. She and Alice B. Toklas stayed at Wilder's apartment while she was lecturing at the university there where Wilder was teaching. Gertrude Stein had been at the university a few months earlier in November of 1934 for the performance of her *Four Saints in Three Acts* at the Auditorium Theatre, but apparently she and Wilder had not met then. Later in the summer of 1935 Wilder visited her in Europe, and they became very close friends. She had listened to writers and advised them before she met Wilder, and she did the same for many in the years after; Wilder, too, had other teachers and listeners and an enormous host of acquaintances; among them William Lyon Phelps at Yale, Freud, Lady Sybil Colefax, and on an extended walking tour the boxer Gene Tunney, whose charm was a model for the characterization of George Brush in *Heaven's My Destination,* though Brush is more firmly based on Wilder himself, his brother, and his father. His friendship with Gertrude Stein was a special one. They were so remarkably close that they talked, not altogether seriously perhaps, about writing a book together, surely a rare instance of mutual artistic and personal sympathy for two people who seem, from a distance, at least, and in spite of the numbers of people who surround them, so solitary. She was to plot it, which is significant in the light of the weakness of Wilder's early work and what he learned from her about narration, and he was to write the words. She wrote it herself, of course, and it was *Ida.* Although Gertrude Stein wrote a great many plays and was devoted to the theater, it is not her plays, with the exception possibly of *Four Saints in Three Acts,* so much as the ideas in her essays and the novel *The Making of Americans* that demonstrate her influence in Wilder's work.

In a letter to her in 1935, after he had read the manuscript of *Four in America,* Wilder wrote, "The Grant I followed best of all and it is full of beauties — on religion and war and America." He added, "It's no news to you that I am a slow-poke plodder in some ways, still stuck in the literal XIXth century,"[13] especially in its concept of America and religion. When he wrote the introduction for its publication in 1947, he said:

> Religion, as Miss Stein uses the term, has very little to do with cults and dogma, particularly in America. . . . Religion is what a person knows — knows beyond knowing, knows beyond anyone's power to teach him — about his relation to the existence in which he finds himself.[14]

Religion for Gertrude Stein, as for other American artists, especially Thoreau and Whitman, was intensity in living, an awareness by the self of surrounding life as well as of its own life. Donald Sutherland, in his very fine book about Gertrude Stein's work, wrote that for her

> a saint, whether he does anything or not, exists in and with the universe and shares its life, sustained in existence by the general miracle of the present world. St. Teresa's remark, "Among the cooking pots moves the Lord," is perhaps the most vivid statement of that. The basis of this intimate exaltation over living with the life of the world was of course not, with Gertrude Stein, the Holy Spirit as in Christian theology, even when she used Christian saints and symbols to articulate what she meant, but rather a vital and radical poetic attitude or intuition.[15]

It is precisely this understanding of religion that Wilder uses in *Our Town* — and in *The Merchant of Yonkers* and *The Skin of Our Teeth,* too — when the Stage Manager tells Emily that the saints and poets have some intuition of the wonder of life.

Heaven's My Destination, coming between *The Woman of Andros* and *Our Town,* offers evidence that Wilder understood the difficulties in his early religious position. The epigraph of *Heaven's My Destination* is from *The Woman of Andros:* "Of all the forms of genius, goodness has the longest awkward age." Here Wilder absolutely defines *goodness* as one sort of genius, which is qualified only by its long period of fumbling. The epigraph also connects the two novels. Wilder was writing of his own artistic awkward age for the "kind of work that . . . he would most like to do well": portray religious experience.

The problems George Brush, the hero of the novel, encounters in his attempts to understand his religious impulses, especially with respect to dogma and any particular religious way — for the Andrian speaks the words to a young man who wishes to fit life to a neat plan — are Wilder's fictionalization of his own efforts. When the *Paris Review* interviewer asked Wilder in 1957 about his resemblance to George Brush, Wilder said:

> I came from a very strict Calvinistic father, was brought up partly among missionaries in China, and went to that splendid college at Oberlin at a time when the classrooms and student life carried a good deal of the pious didacticism which would now be called narrow Protestantism. And that book *Heaven's My Destination* is, as it were, an effort to come to terms with those influences.
>
> The comic spirit is given to us in order that we may analyze, weigh and clarify things in us which nettle us, or which we are outgrowing, or trying to reshape. That is a very autobiographical book.[16]

Wilder, however, never gave over the idea of an overtly religious play. In 1955, at the Edinburgh Festival, a new play of his was presented, *The Alcestiad,* called then over Wilder's objections *A Life in the Sun.* Wilder had been obsessed with the idea of Alcestis for more than twenty years. In *The Woman of Andros,* Chrysis says: "Someday . . . we shall understand why we suffer. I shall be among the shades underground and some wonderful hand, some Alcestis, will touch me and will show me the meaning of all these things."[17] Eight years later, in a letter dated September 28, 1938, from Michael Meyerberg, who produced *The Skin of Our Teeth,* an *Alcestiad* on which Wilder had been working is mentioned.

The first and most obvious reason for dwelling at such length on *The Alcestiad* is that the play is a difficult one and is based on precepts not easily explained. The play also has never been published in Eng-

lish, and as a result there is not the public familiarity with it that surrounds Wilder's other plays. It is not likely, moreover, that it will be
published in the near future. Wilder has come to believe that the central part of Alcestis is too difficult for any actress to undertake successfully, and he has based the future of the play on the opera scored for
it by Louise Talma. But the play is an important one, if for no other
reason than that it is almost alone as a serious religious play written by
a contemporary American. It is, in addition, the culmination of much
of what Wilder tries to say in the theater.

Wilder has a particular interest in the classical Greek theater which
The Alcestiad superficially resembles, especially the plays of Sophocles
because of their religious intensity. He wrote in the introduction to
Francis Storr's translation of *Oedipus Rex,* published in 1955:

> The *Oedipus Rex* opens at the moment that the "other world" has
> chosen to intervene in human affairs, to set in motion the train of events
> that will bring to light the enormities in Oedipus' past. The action of
> *Macbeth* and *Hamlet* is likewise instituted by supernatural agencies,
> but the witches and the ghost of Hamlet's father are easily understood
> as externalizations of the promptings within the protagonists' minds.
> In the Greek plays, however, the gods are objective forces and the audi-
> ence received the anguish of Oedipus and the suicide of Iocasta as being
> required by a power greater and "other" than subjective fancy, and
> under a necessity more significant than the hereditary curse which
> Sophocles has elevated to a larger fatality, the cleansing will of Apollo.[18]

He wrote earlier in the same introduction:

> There has been little religious drama in Europe since the Greeks, and
> the theatre has lost one of its most powerful effects — the shudder and
> awe induced by the presence of the numinous, by the *tremendum* of
> religious experience.[19]

Wilder had outgrown forever the impulse to sermonize. His purpose
was to focus man against the background of the unknown, to reintro-
duce "the presence of the numinous." The problem was how to do it.

After the war, about 1945, Wilder first read seriously the work of
Sören Kierkegaard. It is not surprising, since Kierkegaard's writing
has had a tremendous effect on twentieth-century thought, that Wil-

der, especially with his interest in religion, should have come under his influence. Moreover, Walter Lowrie, the Kierkegaard scholar and translator, was a friend. What is surprising, perhaps, is that Wilder should have emerged from his study of Kierkegaard with a clearer view of religion as he had already learned it from Gertrude Stein but also with as strong a hold as ever on his optimistic view of the human situation. The more fashionable attitude toward Kierkegaard's philosophy is a pessimistic one, led by the writers in the history of Existentialism. Earlier, of course, Wilder had returned from his study of *Finnegans Wake,* largely a pessimistic book, with a cheerful commentary on it, *The Skin of Our Teeth.*

Before Wilder had completed *The Alcestiad,* he published *The Ides of March,* which also resulted from his study of Kierkegaard.[20] The immediate connection between the novel and *The Alcestiad* is that a summary of the first act of the play appears in the novel as part of a version "of the so-called '*Alcestiad of Catullus.*' " One of the fundamental questions raised by the play is directly related to the argument of *The Ides of March:* Do man's actions indeed depend on God, or are they meaningless movements in a void? Wilder told a magazine interviewer that the motto of *The Ides of March*

> is from Goethe's "Faust," a passage . . . freely translated as: Out of man's recognition in fear and awe that there is an unknowable comes all that is best in the explorations of his mind — even though that recognition is often misled into superstition, enslavement, and overconfidence.[21]

His gloss of Goethe as "Out of man's recognition in fear and awe that there is an Unknowable" is remarkably close to the English title of one of Kierkegaard's most famous works, *Fear and Trembling.* Wilder said also:

> The book attempts to show the mind of a man like Julius Caesar, with enormous experience of men and affairs, trying to separate the elements of superstition from those of religion . . . and attempting to ascertain whether his great role in the Roman state was of his own making or whether he was the instrument of a Destiny Force beyond his knowledge.[22]

Wilder's words about Caesar might describe Hercules in *The Alcestiad*. After Alcestis dies, Hercules arrives from his labor of killing the Hydra. He doubts his descent from Zeus; he doubts that the god has any part in his achievement. The doubt creates within him two contradictory feelings. One, he is proud and concludes that he must be a "good man" to have accomplished so great a task. Two, he is reduced to Kierkegaard's fear and trembling, for if the god has no part in his work, then it is meaningless and he can comprehend nothing. His concern is that "someone will come to me and ask me to . . . descend into the Underworld, into Hell . . . and bring back someone who has died."[23] He has come to seek the answer to his doubts from Alcestis.

Wilder has manipulated with great economy and originality the facts of the legend into a complex situation. Hercules is faced with the problem of whether he is able to act through the intercession of divine power or whether his mighty acts are accidents. In the myth there is no question of Hercules' semidivinity; but if the Hercules in Wilder's play is to be regarded as a real man, then his question is one for all of us. Alcestis, who is repeatedly given the epithet of "the silent" and who is indeed silent in death when Hercules arrives, ironically will provide the answer to Hercules by requiring him to do exactly what he fears most: to go down into Hell and bring back someone who has died. The situation provides a dramatization of Kierkegaard's idea that from submitting in fear and trembling to what seems to be the loss of everything, paradoxically everything is returned, and, further, it is given meaning.

Hercules resolves, because of his love for Alcestis, to return her from death. Calling upon Apollo for new strength, he recognizes his dependence on the god, but he understands also that the gods and men must act together. What they can do is what Jesus, for example, totally divine and at the same time totally human, accomplished: the paradoxical death of Death. Alcestis is returned to the living.

Hercules' shift from doubt to faith is unclear, although the situation that prompted it is developed step by step. Wilder encountered the same problem that Eliot raised in *Murder in the Cathedral*. In that play Thomas Becket overcomes the Tempters to announce, "Now is my way clear, now is the meaning plain," but Eliot was unable to

dramatize Thomas' decision. Thomas is in doubt; a long chorus is recited; the doubt is resolved. The resolution remains a mystery. What
Kierkegaard calls "infinite resignation," or the renunciation of everything dearest in the world without, however, denying one's delight in
it, is the last step prior to faith. He wrote that the "secret in life is that
everyone must sew [the shirt of infinite resignation] ... for himself."[24]
Faith itself is merely a witness, never a teacher; one may observe it and
its consequences without understanding what it is. Such a decision as
that reached by Hercules can be dramatized only through the "infinite
resignation," but the decision to faith itself can never be dramatized,
for it is lonely and inexplicable, and, as Kierkegaard wrote, it never
becomes *publici juris,* as the theater is inevitably.

Wilder did not shrink from the difficulties inherent in what he was
presenting. Holding on to the view that faith is a witness, he dramatized as much as he dared, so that the audience might apprehend the
greatness and terror of Hercules' decision, even if they were aware that
such a decision was beyond analytical comprehension.

Upon learning of Alcestis' death, Hercules is moved to a terrible
anger. The concealment of the death, although by Alcestis' wish, was
unfriendly in a most profound way. Hercules shouts:

> I am not a man, since my best friend [Admetus] will not treat me as
> a man ... if I am not fit to share the grief of my friends. . . . For you,
> I am an animal, a stupid animal who goes about killing animals! You
> think I have no mind or heart or soul![25]

In his anger Hercules asserts his humanity, but his anger represents
more than simply the classical plea for the sound mind in a sound
body, with an attempt to clear up any doubts about the quality of the
mind. The accusation he hurls against Admetus is one he might have
made against himself. It is another way of expressing the doubt he
has concerning his own humanity and his relation with the god. Is he
merely an animal, or is he a man with a man's knowledge?[26]

Hercules risks all that is dear in the world — life itself — for an
ideal, his platonic love for Alcestis; but in the same act he regains all
that is dear — life — made dearer and provided with meaning by his
recognition of his relationship with the god. No question ever arises

that the god exists; but his existence is not without its ironies, nor is it a reason for easy comfort. God, in the person of Apollo, opens the play as in the plays of Euripides. He is taunted by Death:

> When the Gods come near to men, sooner or later someone is killed and the kingdom of Death is the richer.
>
> Leave these human beings alone. Stay up on Mount Olympus where you belong, and enjoy yourselves. I've watched this foolishness coming over you for a long time. You made these creatures and then you became infatuated with them — You've thrown the whole world into confusion and it's getting worse every day. All you do is torment them. . . . They will never understand your language, — how can they? The more you try to say something, the more you drive them distraught. . . . Go back to Olympus where you belong. All this loving — It's hard to tell which is the unhappier: *you* or these wretched creatures. When you try to come into their lives you're like a giant in a small room: with every movement you break something. Since you made the mistake of giving them freedom, you must pay the price of being unintelligible.[27]

Death is not wrong, but his view is shortsighted. He is the spokesman for the sophisticated twentieth-century concept of the gods.[28] Death, for his own security, would have the gods remain remote from man. The insistence by Wilder on the recognition that man is in relation with God is hard; it leads to confusion, doubt, and hardship. As the way of the world goes, such a vision of religion is a melancholy one.

Tiresias, when he comes to Thessaly, echoes the danger indicated by Death. After he announces that Apollo will spend one year as a herdsman for Admetus, he says: "Of course there's peril, imbecile. When THEY [the gods] draw near it is always peril."[29] Admetus protests that Apollo has always loved Thessaly, and Tiresias angrily answers:

> Yes, — love, love, love. Let them keep their love to themselves. Look at me: five–six hundred years old and I am not allowed to die. If the Gods didn't love men, we'd all be happy; and the other way round is true, too: if we men didn't love the Gods, we'd all be happy.[30]

Man might be happy without love, but he would also be without that freedom that makes him a man and not an animal. Only through faith is the paradox of the pain of God's love resolved. *The Alcestiad* attempts to show in part what that resolution means to modern man. Apollo's answer to Death is that he has come to earth "to set a song in motion — a story"[31] that will have a lesson for Death. That story is the play itself.

The action of Hercules and its place in the story set in motion by Apollo are clearer when they are regarded in relation with Alcestis, whose complement Hercules is. As her story begins in the first act, she is within Kierkegaard's concept of despair in her refusal to recognize the necessity for the finite. Hercules, on the other hand, was frightened of his relationship with the infinite. Alcestis is to marry Admetus, but she longs instead to serve the god at Delphi and has decided not to marry at all. Her decision is interrupted by the arrival of Tiresias with his message, followed by his introduction of the four uncouth and dirty herdsmen, one of whom is supposed to be Apollo. She is repelled by their appearance, but she speaks to them.

> You [Apollo] know that I have wished to live only for you. — To learn — to be taught by you — the meaning of our life....
>
> Are we human beings to be left without any sign, any word? Are we abandoned? ...
>
> Then we must find our way by ourselves ... and life is a meaningless grasping at this and that ... it is a passionate nonsense.[32]

Alcestis voices her despair in her fear that life is without meaning. One of the herdsmen speaks to her and describes the other three and himself, each of whom has one of Apollo's attributes: healer, singer, pathfinder, and bringer of light. The herdsman denies that any of them is the god. "But," he adds,

> if they did not [*sic?*] exist, these Gods, — *how* would they speak to us? They were there before time began and will be there beyond all time. ... Why, there are some who even say that they *love* us. Could you understand *that*? Love? What kind of love is that, when there is so great a gulf between the lover and the beloved? ...
>
> That would be an unhappy love, — no doubt about that....
>
> ... For if They showed themselves to us in Their glory, it would kill us. If they came to us in a disguise, that would be condescension, — and surely lovers are equal, or they are nothing. ...

I did have an idea this morning: maybe, there is another way — a way to bridge that gulf [between man and the gods], I mean — maybe, for They can do all things, maybe They can find a way to bring those they love *up* — up nearer to them. If Tiresias is right, Apollo is here *divided up* among several people, or many people — four herdsmen and others: Take Admetus, for example . . . slowly I began to see that King Admetus has something that all those other heroes hasn't got. . . . The world changes; it changes slowly. What good would this world be, princess, unless new *kinds* of men came into it — and new kinds of women? . . .

And wouldn't that be, maybe, the way those unhappy lovers — would try to throw a bridge across that gulf I was talking about?[33]

In this speech is an infinitely more interesting concept of love as the bridge than in *The Bridge of San Luis Rey.* Tiresias is certainly correct in his explanation of love as pain, but he is truly blind in that he cannot see what the pain means and that it is possible only through much joy. A man can love God by loving what is good in man, but like Pamphilus in *The Woman of Andros,* he must learn to "praise all living, the bright and the dark."

Wilder has dramatized in the four herdsmen more than the idea, which is become almost sentimental, that every man is in part divine. Aglaia, Alcestis' nurse, warns, "I hope you don't think of them [the gods] as people!"[34] Man has no part in God; he exists *before* God, and this existence gives man his identity. However, "Out of love," Kierkegaard wrote:

> God becomes man. . . . As man He assumes the lowly form of a serv-
> ant. He expresses what it is to be a lowly man, to the intent that no one
> shall think himself excluded, or think that it is human prestige or pres-
> tige among men which brings one nearer to God. No, he is the lowly
> man.[35]

Kierkegaard has described the act of Jesus, of course, but he also describes Apollo's act in Wilder's play. The very existence of the four herdsmen provides a meaning for life, for they represent God's love for man. God "comprehends (*comprehendit*) reality itself, all the individuals; for Him the individual is not subsumed under the concept."[36] The duty of man, as the shepherd hints and Kierkegaard explicitly defines, is to love finitude, or ordinary reality, as well as infinitude, or that which is mysterious.

Alcestis had been the person described by Kierkegaard under the heading "The Despair of Infinitude is due to the lack of Finitude."

> The self thus leads a fantastic existence in abstract endeavor after infinity [Alcestis' longing to serve at Delphi] . . . constantly lacking itself, from which it merely gets further and further away. So, for example, in the religious sphere. The God-relationship infinitizes; but this may so carry a man away that it becomes an inebriation, it may seem to a man as though it were unendurable to exist before God — for the reason that a man cannot return to himself, cannot become himself. Such a fantastic religious individual would say, . . . "That a sparrow can live is comprehensible; it does not know anything about existing before God. But to know that one exists before God — and then not to go crazy or be brought to naught!"[37]

Alcestis' fear that life is a "passionate nonsense" is exactly the cry of the fantastic religious individual. She must learn to become herself, to return to herself — in *Finitude*. The herdsmen bear witness to God's incarnation in the lowly man and teach her the way she may accomplish becoming herself. Simple, daily existence has its meaning before God; Alcestis learns the way and the value of daily living or finitude. After her death she is described as a servant, and Admetus says that she had called herself "the servant of servants"; the term *servant* is applied frequently by Kierkegaard to Jesus.

Before Alcestis can answer the herdsman, Admetus comes to her and gives her permission to leave him, but he says, "When such love [as his for Alcestis] is not met by a love in return, then life is itself a deception."[38] Alcestis recognizes, and so should the audience recognize, that the way to bridge the gulf between man and God is to love life, for her to love Admetus.

Alcestis replies to Admetus:

> Ask me to love all the things that you love . . . and to be queen of your Thessaly. Ask me in pain to bear you children. To walk beside you at the great festivals. To comfort you when you are despairing. To make sure that when you return from a journey the water for your bath will be hot, and that your house, Admetus, will be as well-ordered as your

> mind. To live for you and for your children and for your people, — To live for you as though every moment I were ready to die for you — so gladly, so readily to die for you.[39]

The meaning of life is revealed in living — hot bath water as well as great festivals — and that living must be done with an awareness that it can cease at any time. Life must not be lived as though it were a mere passage to something better. It cannot be embraced with reservation. The sorrow is that it has no permanence. The daily awareness of the possibility of losing life is close to Kierkegaard's view of the life in dread. Alcestis has despaired over the meaning of life because she has averted herself from living in her desire to understand it in God. Her love for Admetus brings with it an awareness of the sorrow for life's impermanence, and ironically that sorrow increases immeasurably the value of life.

A message from Delphi comes to Alcestis in the second act, informing her that Admetus, who is dying, can be saved if someone else desires to die in his place. Several people offer to do the act, including one of the herdsmen, who is himself the cause of Admetus' sickness, but Alcestis recognizes that the message is for her alone. She is the dramatization of infinite resignation. In writing of this infinite resignation, Kierkegaard observed:

> For it is great to give up one's wish, but it is greater to hold it fast after having given it up, it is great to grasp the eternal, but it greater to hold fast to the temporal after having given it up.[40]

Alcestis desires to die, but she is the more strongly attached to life.

> I *hate* to die. . . . I must die from Admetus. I must die from my children. I must die from this sunlight.[41]

She knows, too, that her sacrifice must be inspired by love for it to be, in the religious sense of Kierkegaard, a trial. Otherwise, it is a base temptation, as she explains to the herdsman that his death would be. To the herdsman, dying would be an easy way of avoiding his guilt for having been the cause of Admetus' sickness. Alcestis has learned, too, that paradoxically what she does for God she does for herself. She will be saving Admetus, and through her overwhelming love for him, for life, she will have bridged the gulf between the gods and man.

Alcestis' sacrifice has one very important consequence: the action of Hercules or the defeat of Death. Kierkegaard, in describing the sacrifice of Jesus for all mankind, wrote:

> Ah, wretched is the man who never has felt the urge of compelling love to sacrifice everything out of love, and who accordingly has not been able to do it! But then when he discovered that precisely this sacrifice of his out of love might possibly occasion the other, the loved one, the greatest unhappiness — what then? Then either love within him lost its resilience, from being a life of power collapsed into the introverted rumination of a sad sentiment, his was a deserter to love, he did not venture to perform this work of love, himself sinking down, not under this work, but under the weight of this possibility. For just as a weight is infinitely heavier when it is attached to the end of a rod and the man who lifts it has to hold the opposite end, so every work becomes infinitely harder when it becomes dialectic, so that what love prompts one to do for the beloved, care for the beloved seems again in another sense to dissuade from doing. — Or else love conquered, and he ventured to do this work out of love. Oh, but in the joyfulness of love (as love always is joyful, especially when it sacrifices all) there was nevertheless a deep sorrow — for this sad result indeed was possible. Behold, he therefore brought to completion this work of love, he offered the sacrifice (in which for his part he exulted), but not without tears. Over this — what shall I call it? — historical painting of inward life there hovered that dark possibility. And yet, if this had not hovered over it, his work would not have been the work of true love.[42]

Alcestis' sacrifice, then, made in joy, essentially to create joy, carries with it the burden of potential sorrow — the sorrow of those who love her. The arrival of Hercules, as in the myth, prevents by Alcestis' command any sign of mourning. Even when her death is revealed, Hercules is moved to anger and Admetus to apology. Nor is any sorrow aroused in the audience. Wilder has deliberately eschewed tears, heeding Kierkegaard's reminder of the words of Jesus, "Blessed is he who shall not be offended in me."[43] Kierkegaard's final comment on the sacrifice from love is to quote Plutarch: "From men man learns to speak, from the Gods to keep silent."[44] Alcestis is silent in death, as she was called in life "the silent."

The third act is twenty years later. Alcestis has not been returned from the dead to live happily ever after. Unlike Euripides' play, where Alcestis is joined again with Admetus and two rather foolish and selfish people are given another opportunity to live their lives together with better grace, Wilder's play examines carefully just what happened. A plague is raging. Admetus is dead. Alcestis is truly a servant in the palace of the conquering king Agis, who has killed Admetus and two of Alcestis' children. Death and Apollo meet again, and Apollo warns Death that the ray of light that entered the Kingdom of Death with the rescue of Alcestis will be multiplied beyond all counting by men to come. Ironically, for this to happen, for the final death of Death, ruin and havoc are also necessary, for, as Apollo says, "death has a large part in every good story."[45]

Epimenes, the sole remaining son of Alcestis and Admetus, and his friend Cheriander return in disguise during the plague to establish justice in Thessaly, to commit murder and butchery, presumably to kill Agis and re-establish the family of Admetus on the throne. They plan to gain admission with the false report of Epimenes' death. This situation is similar to any of a number in Greek legend, but the similarity ends with this beginning. Alcestis persuades them that they are needed to help in the struggle against the pestilence that is raging. With that, Agis enters in mourning, for his beloved daughter, Laodarnia, is sick with the plague. Laodarnia dies, and Agis in anguish first wishes to die himself and then to rescue Laodarnia as Hercules did Alcestis. Alcestis tells him:

> The bitterness of death, Agis, is *past* pain, — but that is not all. The last bitterness of death is not parting — though that is great grief. I died once. It is not even ceasing to be. What is the last bitterness of death, King Agis? . . . It is the despair that one has not lived. It is the despair that one's life has been without meaning — or worse still: has almost had a meaning. That it has been nonsense — happy or unhappy — that it has been senseless.[46]

When Agis protests that Laodarnia had loved him, Alcestis replies, "Love is not the meaning. It is only one of the signs that there is a meaning."[47] Wilder never tells what the meaning is. "No one of us can tell that to another."[48] The play, however, dramatically shows what that meaning might be: to be oneself by coming into relation with God. For Alcestis it was revealed partly by living and dying for Admetus. Agis' despair is his refusal to be comforted in the face of Laodarnia's death. He clings to her dying almost as a way to remember her; her death is his identity. Despair, however, is necessary preparation to self-recognition. Agis was unable to understand the error of his past life, his murdering, until he himself suffered.

Alcestis, who finds the end of her journey in Apollo's grove, is a witness, Kierkegaard's knight of faith. The knight is described in detail.

> He is no genius. . . . He lives as carefree as a ne'er-do-well, and yet he buys up the acceptable time at the dearest price, for he does not do the least thing except by virtue of the absurd. . . . With infinite resignation he has drained the cup of life's profound sadness, he knows the bliss of the infinite, he senses the pain of renouncing everything, the dearest things he possesses in the world, and yet finiteness tastes to him just as good as to one who never knew anything higher. . . . He resigned everything infinitely, and then he grasped everything again by virtue of the absurd. He constantly makes the movements of infinity, but he does this with such correctness and assurance that he constantly gets the finite out of it . . . to be able to fall down in such a way that the same second it looks as if one were standing and walking, to transform the leap of life into a walk, *absolutely to express the sublime in the pedestrian* — . . . this is the one and only prodigy.[49]

Wilder's efforts since *Heaven's My Destination* have all been directed toward expressing "the sublime in the pedestrian." Alcestis is the knight of faith, but who can understand her? The audience can only watch her and do their best with their own lives. *The Alcestiad* is unqualifiedly and unwaveringly, with no "concession to a contemporary standard of good manners,"[50] a religious play. The meaning of life that Wilder has cherished so carefully throughout all his work

finally found its clearest expression through the philosophy of Kierkegaard. Wilder, in an address on the Blashfield Foundation of the
American Academy of Arts and Letters in 1948, said:

> Another mode open to us is to accept a Time of Troubles as an outward
> expression of an incoherence of man's inner life — and that such an in-
> coherence is an eternal condition — is indeed, a norm. This view has
> high authority. Matthew Arnold quoted with approval Goethe's re-
> mark that "the Iliad teaches us that it is our task here on earth to enact
> Hell daily." For our times the principal exponent of this view is Sören
> Kierkegaard. His description of the basic absurdity of man's relation to
> the universe has enjoyed an ever-increasing influence in our time. Out
> of that absurdity he made and counsels, the leap of faith; but Kierke-
> gaard's "faith by paradox" . . . does not sound like the faith we have
> associated with ages of security. For him the leap of faith cannot take
> place without an acknowledgment of one's life in dread. It is naturally
> a doctrine of this school that those persons who are not aware of this
> tension in themselves are merely immature and that a culture which
> does not exhibit it is either childlike or hypocritical or consciously play-
> acting — pretending that there is no dread, no absurdity, no leap, and
> no need for an explanation of experience. . . .
>
> The artist [unlike the philosopher] is under no such compulsion to
> supply final answers and to balance the books of good and evil. . . . If,
> as Goethe says, it is our duty in these times and in all times to enact Hell
> daily, it is sufficient for the artist that he describe such a life. Ages of
> Security and Anxiety look much alike to him.[51]

Here is in part Wilder's credo as an artist. Although *The Alcestiad* is
clearly religious, it provides no answers; it does not seek to comfort the
audience with soothing reports of rewards waiting for the good or
anyone else. It is religious in the sense of Gertrude Stein's cooking
pots, of Goethe's reading of the *Iliad,* or Kierkegaard's understanding
of the stories of Job and Abraham and Isaac. Existence is difficult, painfully so; but it is available and better than anyone can realize.

As the epigraph to this chapter states, Thornton Wilder believes
that the religious impulses in man are enduring. They may assume
different forms at different times and different places, but what they
mean is common to all men. Wilder turned his attention to the idea

of living, which underlies all human life. He discovered for himself that man's relation to the unknowable, to the divine, helps clarify the meaning behind this idea of living. It is not surprising, then, that he should have emphasized the independence of these two interrelated aspects of human experience from time and space. But that is a further problem.

III

ALL TIMES AND ALL PLACES

---

*The human adventure is much the same
in all times and all places.*

KNOWING that he can never have it (and probably that he does not really want it), the American still gazes wistfully at the European's identification with time and place.[1] Norman Holmes Pearson has described the American writer's longing for community as "the desire to belong, not so much to any particular society as to a spiritual fellowship which unites men with each other."[2] Wilder more generally contrasted the European with the American.

> "I am I," says the European, "because the immemorial repetitions of my country's way of life surround me. I know them and they know me."
>
> An American can have no such stabilizing relation to any one place, nor to any one community, nor to any one moment in time.[3]

The European understands his time and place literally; the American tries to realize his life in terms of an idea. His community is located in the imagination.

Wilder's lifelong traveling from place to place has encouraged him to regard geography as essentially without any real influence on identity. But his is the American experience — Sartre has called our cities mere camps, temporary and fragile — exaggerated. Time also has a special meaning for Wilder. In 1954 he wrote:

> After I'd graduated from college I was sent to Europe to study archaeology. One day our class in Rome was taken out into the country

to dig up a bit of the Etruscan world, a street. Once thousands of persons had walked it. The rut was very deep. Those who have uncovered such a spot are never the same again.

Now in the 20th Century, we all have something of the mind of an archaeologist. The other centuries knew that many people had lived and died a long while ago, and they knew there were many people living on the earth. But the invention of the printing press . . . had made these realizations far more actual. Now everybody knows them, not as something you learn in school and recite to one another, but "in their bones" — that millions and billions have lived and died. The extent of this enlarged realization alters the whole view of life.[4]

Wilder's first novel, *The Cabala,* literally translated into plot what the archaeologist finds, by exposing at once several important layers in the history of Rome. John Keats lives alongside a Renaissance princess, whose son embodies some of the spirit of classical Rome, and the actual time of the novel is sometime during the first quarter of the twentieth century. This view of the simultaneous presentness of all the past Wilder had encountered already as early as his days at Oberlin where a teacher, Charles Wager, told him, "Every great work was written this morning."[5]

Yet if Wilder feels these problems as an American, he feels them as strongly as a man who wants to write for the stage. In "Some Thoughts on Playwriting," he contrasted the novel with the play:

> The novel is a past reported in the present. On the stage it is always now. This confers upon the action an increased vitality which the novelist longs in vain to incorporate into his work. . . .
> *A play is what takes place.*
> *A novel is what one person tells us took place.*[6]

Gertrude Stein's book *The Geographical History of America,* for which Wilder wrote the introduction, helped Wilder to understand his own experience in the light of all experience. In 1935 he wrote to Gertrude Stein:

> What a book! I mean What a book! I've been living for a month with ever-increasing intensity on the conceptions of Human Nature and the Human Mind, and on the relations of Masterpieces to their apparent

subject matter. Those things, yes and identity, have become cell and marrow in me and now at last I have more about them. . . .

Yes, I'm crazy about America. And you did that to me, too.[7]

If Wilder was crazy about America, it was not simply patriotic feeling. In the *Time* magazine cover story in 1953, he is quoted as saying about *The Geographical History:*

Human nature, she [Gertrude Stein] said, clings to identity, to location in time and place. The human mind has no identity; it gazes at pure existing and pure creating, and "it knows what it knows when it knows it." It can be found in masterpieces, for masterpieces alone report the ever-unfolding and the boundless Now. But it can also be found in America, which was brought up to believe in boundlessness. America's very geography, said Stein, is "an invitation to wander."[8]

All great literature of the past, myths, and history are meaningful and belong to the present of twentieth-century America despite their apparently ephemeral and particularizing characters. In fact, what is particular about them is lost as Americans struggle to make the "masterpieces" their own; it is as though all the past were one great American myth. This is another way of expressing Professor Pearson's "spiritual fellowship which unites men with each other," as opposed to a "particular society." The history of Europe, for example, is real for Americans, but in the sense that a myth is real: what it says is addressed to the Human Mind; the events themselves are relevant only insofar as they convey meaning.

Gertrude Stein's Human Nature and the Human Mind are related to Wilder's idea of "each tiny occasion of the daily life and the vast stretches of time and place."[9] He told the *Paris Review* interviewer:

The Skin of Our Teeth, which takes five thousand years to go by, is really a way of trying to make sense out of the multiplicity of the human race and its affections.

So that I see myself making an effort to find the dignity in the trivial of our daily life, against those preposterous stretches which seem to rob it of any such dignity; and the validity of each individual's emotion.[10]

Human Nature in *Our Town* is found in each of the small events located in turn-of-the-century New England and in *The Skin of Our*

Teeth in the events of a particular suburban family, but because of the peculiar style of generalized presentation of "pure existing and pure creating," that is, the absence or the confusion of time and place, it results in an appeal to the Human Mind. Wilder learned from Gertrude Stein that the qualities most characteristically American are those most appealing to the Human Mind.

Wilder paid part of his debt to Gertrude Stein in *Our Town*. Throughout the play he constantly reminds the audience that what they are witnessing happened a long time ago. Grover's Corners, New Hampshire, never existed except as a dreamy bucolic idyll that is desired but not realized. The Stage Manager helps convey the nostalgia through memory when he says, "First automobile's going to come along in about five years — belonged to banker Cartwright."[11] When Mrs. Gibbs appears on stage for the first time, the Stage Manager says:

> Mrs. Gibbs died first — long time ago, in fact. She went out to visit her daughter, Rebecca, who married an insurance man in Canton, Ohio, and died there — pneumonia — but her body was brought back here. She's up in the cemetery there now — in with a whole mess of Gibbses and Herseys — she was Julia Hersey 'fore she married.[12]

After the newspaper boy, Joe Crowell, goes offstage:

> Want to tell you something about that boy Joe Crowell there. Joe was awful bright — graduated from high school here, head of his class. So he got a scholarship to Massachusetts Tech. Graduated head of his class there, too. It was all wrote up in the Boston paper at the time. Goin' to be a great engineer, Joe was. But the war broke out and he died in France. — All that education for nothing.[13]

Mrs. Gibbs is one of the many Herseys and Gibbses, before and after her, as she lies in the cemetery. The same is true of Joe Crowell. He is one of the many whose promise was wasted in catastrophe, whether natural or man-made, although perhaps Joe is seen more as a sacrifice than as a waste, for presumably he died defending the things represented by the best in *Our Town*.

The glimpses of future time — that is, time after the action of the play but before the time of the audience — reminders that what happens is actually time past, are more than inverse flashbacks. They rep-

resent, like the sudden return on the wedding day to George's proposal
to Emily, a consistent and deliberate rearrangement of time. The logic
that dominates the play has little relation to the progression of historical time, although Wilder reminds the audience that as individuals
they must all finally submit to the tyranny of that historical time.
Partly Wilder relies on this confusion, as with the interruption by the
proposal, to prevent the ordinariness of subject matter from seeming
uninteresting. More importantly, however, the interruption of events
without having any of them reach a conclusion — George never really
gets around to proposing to Emily — prevents them, and their place
as one in a great number, from being overlooked. They are never one
part of a sequence, but always stand out in their own separateness.

The reminder of time past seems to work directly in opposition to
Wilder's idea of the stage's eternal *now;* however, as memory it moves
with a logic all its own and exists as present time. He said in 1952 in
a magazine article, "The American Loneliness," "Time is something
we create, we call into being, not something we submit to — an order
outside us."[14] By recalling past time, Wilder has, in the three acts of
his play, created his own time separate from that time of the audience
which ticks away each minute. He has presented in recognizable sequence birth, marriage, and death, events analogous to the cycle of
life of any member of the audience. But the sequence — particularly
its end in death — gives the events a special poignancy, and the events
achieve a meaning beyond the sequence. Each event in the life of
Emily Webb is single and unimportant, but more, each event is also
part of a universe too vast to imagine. The repeated shifts in time are
reminders that all parts of life's sequence are in operation for any
number of people at any time. It is the force of memory that is always
in the present tense. This memory, juggling all the events at once like
a circus performer, keeps the action in the eternal *now* on stage. Wilder offers memory as the real thing, feeling that it has a greater value
than the actual experience. Witnessing the past with all the advantages
of hindsight but without the power to change anything dramatizes
the anguish of the inadequacy of life.

Emily in the third act, when she is dead, sees beyond mortality the
continuity of life. The audience, too, should see themselves as having

a place in a great continuum. When the Stage Manager says that those people who dig up the bank's cornerstone will know more about the people of *Our Town* "than the Treaty of Versailles and the Lindbergh flight,"[15] he is saying the same thing as Emily in a different way — that the events of history have to do with time, but the *real* life of the people is immortal. "Yet [in Babylon] every night all those families sat down to supper, and the smoke went up the chimney — same as here."[16] Although the dead forget, and however inadequate humanity may be, life goes on eternally in the same old way.

For *The Skin of Our Teeth,* Wilder devised a single complex time from three distinct points of measurement, sometimes shifting from one to the other, sometimes fusing them with one another. The first and simplest use of time is that which measures the events of the Antrobus family, living as any suburban family in the United States of the mid-twentieth century. This is the family of numberless situation comedies. Along with this artificial present time is historical time — the family through history. So that the past might gain an even greater relevance to the present, Wilder exploited the stage time, the two hours it takes the play to be performed, by having the actors pretend to be actors who are performing a play. Underlying these is a thematic progression, like the birth to death of *Our Town.* The first disaster the Antrobus family encounters is purely physical and from outside, the Ice Age. The flood of the second act is also physical and from outside, but with the implication that it results from some sort of moral failing on man's part. The third and least comic, war, is exclusively man's effort to destroy himself. Yet each time man has it within his power to retrieve his situation from destruction at the last moment and to begin again.

In the first act, Moses, one of the refugees from the approaching glacier, questions Mrs. Antrobus about her family: "I understand you had two sons." She turns to the audience: "Abel, Abel, my son, my son, Abel, my son, Abel, Abel, my son."[17] The pain of the loss of children to parents complexly superimposed on murder or fratricide, really the same things in a view that regards man as a single family, is deftly and movingly expressed through the cultural memory of Cain and Abel and further of David and Absalom. The mood of complicated sorrows is interrupted at once by a comic shriek from Sabina in the kitchen. The comedy prevents Mrs. Antrobus from appearing simply a maudlin bore, but it is to the point, for Sabina has seen Henry, or Cain, the other son, throw a stone at a neighbor's boy. Although Sabina is funny, what she sees — "And it looked to me like stark murder"[18] — is horrifying enough; man never seems to have learned very much from his past mistakes.

Again when the Antrobus family, re-enacting the story of Noah at Atlantic City, are climbing aboard the ark, Henry is nowhere to be found. Mrs. Antrobus on the boardwalk frantically calls him, and then in desperation, switching from the name Henry, she calls Cain. Henry suddenly appears. The substitution of names and the almost magical appearance of Henry combine to make a frightening piece of stage business. Mrs. Antrobus, the incarnation of selfless mother love, refuses to leave without Henry, who is everything that is disgusting and detestable in man. Not only is Henry loved in spite of his wickedness, but because man is not human without being evil, Henry must go along into the ark. There is even some relief in the audience as the lost child is found; "Here I am, mama," he says brightly. That he is called by love suggests an aspect in man almost too private and sinister to be presented any other way but fictionally, if it is not to be sentimental or false.

In Act III the audience see the culmination of Henry's career. Sabina, now the returning camp-follower, attempts to force Mrs. Antrobus and Gladys to recognize that Henry is the enemy. Upon his return, however, Henry is given one of the two baked potatoes being saved for Mr. Antrobus and is nourished back to health despite his unchanged ways. He snarls, "The first thing to do is to burn up those old books; it's the ideas he [Antrobus] gets out of those old books . . . that makes the whole world so you can't live in it."[19] At best, Moses and Homer are refugees and the Muses a pathetic singing troupe in America. Although on the fringes, they are there available to us in our need. Henry, a book-burner, would destroy them utterly. Antrobus, his father, is also hated. "I'll kill him so fast. I've spent seven years trying to find him; the others I've killed were just substitutes."[20] Wilder has called up the Oedipal father-son competition, but it is not the usual Freudian cliché. Henry's urge is to self-destruction, to tear from himself all that is best and most productive in the past history of mankind. Here is the answer to Mrs. Antrobus' call to him from the boardwalk. He is all evil in all time, retained and *cherished* in the family unit. The audience can expect nothing different.

Having the characters in the play played by actors who are also characters in the play permits Wilder to speak directly and in a somewhat didactic manner to the audience, much as the Stage Manager does in *Our Town*. As actors miss their cues and are taken ill, as Sabina refuses to say her lines and confides in the audience in the character of the actress Miss Somerset, and as the scenery totters out of place, the play, like the human race, seems on the point of collapse. But it, too, will get through by the skin of its teeth. The contretemps in the play's production show that the past lives not only in the present of the family Antrobus but also in the present and the future of each member of the audience; the past is inescapable.

In only one place does the shifting from the particular reality of the Antrobus family to a reality beyond it become obtrusive. After the war Antrobus and Henry struggle together, and their fight develops into a "real" one between the two actors. Wilder felt compelled to provide for these actors psychological explanations for their behavior. It is unfortunate that Sabina should be the spokesman in this scene for the common-sense view that evil needs no psychologizing, for she has been consistently discredited throughout the play, and there is no reason to believe her now. The explanation is unconvincing, a refugee from a social worker's report, with about the same validity and dramatic value. The scene is an even greater surprise since Wilder has always assiduously avoided dependence on the clinic.[21]

The three levels of time are completed in the speeches of the hours and extended both backward and forward by the circular structure of the play. In an article about Joyce in 1954 Wilder wrote about books that are not read, using those of Rousseau as examples.

> Did you ever read Rousseau's *Émile* or *La Nouvelle Héloïse?* I never did — but I can pretty well believe that all of us, whether we know it or not, have been in large part formed by them. Every century has its underground books which have permeated thought. Often they have

been transmitted through relatively few readers. I believe those two great books of Rousseau are shaping us still — though many of us will probably never read them.[22]

The speeches of the hours, a device Wilder had used ten years earlier in *Pullman Car Hiawatha,* demonstrate his belief that the past is alive all around us. History, of whatever sort, is the really important world in which we all live.

Movies have always played fast and loose with time and place through what are now well-worn technical clichés, flashbacks, dissolves, and so on. But when the film of *Our Town* was made, Wilder had some difficulty persuading the studio to abandon its preconceived notions of what the audience would admit and to retain his special attitude toward place. When George Gibbs and Emily Webb marry, for example, it is not the wedding of two particular people from Grover's Corners that Wilder dramatized; it is the wedding of everybody everywhere. He had used New Hampshire and by implication the whole United States for his place, and he knew precisely what he had achieved.

It is amazing that *Our Town* was filmed at all. In the thirties playwrights did not keep quite so keen an eye on Hollywood as the ultimate goal for their efforts as they appear to today. Wilder, like so many others, was the real thing for a while, a script writer for the movies, though he never adapted any of his own work. Alfred Hitchcock's *Shadow of a Doubt* is his only complete script, and one critic has gone so far as to say that the considerable value of the movie in terms particularly of the characterization of the young girl is owed entirely to Wilder. *The Bridge of San Luis Rey* had been a movie, but *Our Town,* which had nearly flopped out of town and might never have reached its tremendous success in New York, did not appear a likely candidate. However, the daughter of a Hollywood executive, acquiring culture and education in one of the best Eastern women's colleges, admired the play and persuaded her father, undoubtedly against his better financial judgment, to transform it to film, if only for the sake of prestige: a rare instance of *ars gratia artis* at work.

Some of the correspondence between Wilder and Sol Lesser, the producer, about the making of the film was published in *Theatre Arts.*

The problem of the opening was discussed at length, and one of the solutions was to have the Stage Manager shown with a jigsaw puzzle of the United States. This was not used finally, but Wilder wrote in its defense:

> Mr. Morgan appearing at the door of his drugstore ... seems to me far less persuasive and useful than the opening over the jigsaw puzzle. The puzzle opening has the advantages:
>
> (1) Of setting the background against the whole United States, that constant allusion to larger dimensions of time and place, which is one of the principal elements of the play; and
>
> (2) Of giving the actor and audience that transitional moment between talking one's thoughts and addressing-a-theatre-audience from the screen, that Sacha Guitry found necessary, too. It would seem to me that each occasion that Mr. Morgan addresses the audience directly should have some such preparation from monologue to address.[23]

In the theater the audience actually see the event unfolding before them. Wilder's attempt to present the *now* so that it is related to all time and does not dwindle into meaninglessness was particularly difficult because Americans have no common point of view, but it is this absence itself that he has set to work for him. He deliberately exploited the invitation to wander offered by America's geography. He has said that the absence of scenery encouraged this relationship of "the ever-unfolding and the boundless Now" to past and future time by removing the particular place.

Wilder has asserted that his apprenticeship for the theater was largely a struggle to overcome the pervasive power of the box set. Commenting on this assertion, Gerald Weales wrote that the battle to splinter the box set had been won by the time Wilder got into it.[24] Although his argument is not untrue, it is misleading. Today if anyone has the strength to look into the New York theaters as one dreary play opens after another week after week during the season, he will see that every production with funds to afford it has one version or another of the box set. When the box set does give way to other kinds of design on Broadway, the idea behind it is usually a trick or display of chic artiness. The various *isms,* of course, employed the stage self-consciously before they found their way from the tyranny of the cash register to the comfort of the classroom or the library shelf. What Weales missed, however, was Wilder's personal fight to escape from the confining realism of the Belasco set he imagined, for example, for *The Trumpet Shall Sound,* without putting on the yoke of a militantly particular vision of the human animal, like that, say, of Expressionism.

Wilder's efforts to expand the stage were intimately involved with his preoccupation with the problems of time and space. He wrote in a preopening puff for *Our Town* in the New York *Times:*

> William James used to warn his students against being impressed by the "abject truth." . . . [Most works in realism tell a succession of such abject truths and] they are deeply in earnest, every detail is true and yet the whole finally tumbles to the ground — true but without significance. . . .
>
> So I tried to restore significance to the small details of life by removing scenery.[25]

When the Stage Manager tells the audience that a new bank is going up in Grover's Corners and in its cornerstone will be placed documents "for people to dig up . . . a thousand years from now," he adds:

> So — people a thousand years from now — this is the way we were in the provinces north of New York at the beginning of the twentieth century. — This is the way we were: in our living and in our dying.[26]

What the audience see is their own lives stripped of all meaningless particularized detail and viewed as though from a thousand years. *Our Town* dramatizes Gertrude Stein's observation in *The Making of Americans:*

> Repeating is the whole of living and by repeating comes understanding, and understanding is to some the most important part of living. Repeating is the whole of living, and it makes of living a thing always more familiar to each one and so we have old men's and old women's wisdom, and repeating, simple repeating is the whole of them.[27]

The relationship between *Our Town* and *The Making of Americans* seems even closer when, seizing on Wilder's hint in the *Times* article, we remember that Gertrude Stein was one of William James's more famous students. Undoubtedly she accepted the warning against the "abject truth" and made it her own.

Wilder has always looked for support and inspiration in the work of other writers, though he transforms what he gathers into a distinctive work of his own. In 1932 he had completed a translation of André Obey's *Le Viol de Lucrèce*. He undertook the task as a labor of love, for he strongly admired Obey's early stage work. His admiration paid dividends in a lesson learned. Lewis Morton, writing in the *American Review* in 1935, said of La Compagnie des Quinze of Jacques Copeau, which was closely associated with Obey's theatrical development, that "they deliberately eschewed whatever smacked of machinery, ornament, display.... With its concrete floor, its bare walls, and the plain wooden pillars of its central colonnade ... [their stage] made no pretense at reality."[28] Wilder incidentally picked up the idea for the Mammoth and the Dinosaur for *The Skin of Our Teeth* from the animals in Obey's *Noé*, but he saw most clearly in Obey's plays the infinite possibilities of the bare stage set to work in a popular theater.

More important as a model for Wilder, because of its humor and its less coldly allegorical qualities, is a strange play that until recently was almost never performed, Alfred Jarry's *Ubu Roi*. At its first performance in December of 1896, beginning with its famous opening word, *merde, Ubu Roi* caused an uproar, mostly for reasons untheatrical; its language and ideas scandalized the audience. Jarry himself said of the play, "La lutte contre le Grand Torteux, d'Ibsen, était passée presque inaperçue."[29] Only later did the play hit with some valuable impact.

In a letter to Lugnée-Poe, the man who mounted *Ubu Roi*, Jarry wrote, suggesting a manner of staging:

> Adoption d'un seul décor, ou mieux, d'un fond uni supprimant les levers et baissers de rideau pendant l'acte unique. Un personnage correctement vêtu viendrait, comme un guignol accrocher un pancarte signifiant le lieu de la scène. (Notez que je suis certain de la supériorité "suggestive" de la pancarte écrite, sur le décor. Un décor, ni une figuration ne rendraient l'armée polonaise en marche dans l'Ukraine.)
>
> Suppression des foules, lesquelles sont souvent mauvaise à la scène et gênent l'intelligence. Ainsi, un seul soldat dans la scène de la revue, un seul dans la bousculade où Ubu dit: "Quel tas de gens, quelle fuite, etc...."

Costume aussi peu couleur locale ou chronologique que possible (ce que rend mieux l'idée d'une chose éternelle); moderne — de préférence, puisque la satire est moderne. . . .

Je ne vous ai parlé d'Ubu Roi que parce qu'il a l'avantage d'être accessible à la majorité du public.[30]

Jarry's suggestion of "un fond uni, supprimant les levers et baissers de rideau" has for its counterpart in *Our Town* the first directions for the scene.

No curtain.
No scenery.
The audience, arriving, sees an empty stage in half-light.[31]

The man bearing the placard to set the scene has his counterpart in the Wilder play in the Stage Manager's location of the town.

The name of the town is Grover's Corners, New Hampshire — just across the Massachusetts line; latitude 42 degrees 40 minutes; longitude 70 degrees 37 minutes. The First Act shows a day in our town. The day is May 7, 1901. The time is just before dawn.[32]

The detailed location seems to provide the town with individuality which it really does not possess. Because of the bare stage, the town is all towns.

The wedding guests and the dead in the cemetery create the illusion of infinite numbers of people, though in fact only very few are there on stage. In a play, one soldier is indeed better than an army. It is important that Jarry emphasized the eternal. Wilder told an interviewer in 1948 that his play "ceased being parochial by dint of using a dramatic method — the absence of representative scenery which intimates the universe."[33] And both writers sought to attract to their theaters the crowd.

Jarry theorized in several essays, most notably in "De L'inutilité du théâtre au théâtre," about the theater and expressed in more detail his attack on Ibsen and realism.[34] His ideas for the theater are flexible and adaptable, for they do not depend on a particular political or social vision of the human animal; they are closer to the basis of drama itself, without demanding any adherence to rigid or specific conventions. He angrily opposed the late nineteenth-century thesis plays, the well-made plays, and the plays of realism. His theoretical destruction of these kinds of drama, however, did not make itself felt in any great way. Jarry's writing has always been considered, because of his personal extravagances, as somewhat of a joke — the work of an eccentric and a crank. But some discerning people — Cocteau, Gide, Apollinaire, and Sacha Guitry among them — did recognize that *Ubu Roi* had succeeded to a greater degree in the struggle against the influence of Ibsen than most of the other experimental drama of the time, for it did not attempt to impose a new set of rules, beyond suggesting that modern realism was a dead end.

Jarry's struggle was primarily directed against the box set, and it is not therefore surprising that he should have aroused Wilder's interest. Wilder utilized Jarry's notions that the spectator in the theater sees what he wants in spite of scenery, with scenery at its best only getting in the way, that great pleasure results from permitting the imagination to work, and that, in fact, the spectator sees "le vrai décor exosmosé sur la scène."[35] In *Our Town* he has even taken Jarry's suggestion that the scenery might be carried like a table. The trellises of the Webb and Gibbs homes, for example, are thrust forward when needed, before the eyes of the audience. These concepts of the stage have been retrieved from the fantastic *Ubu Roi* and set to work among entertainment industry.

Wilder's transportation of Jarry's theatrical ideas to Broadway necessarily changed them. In 1931 Wilder tried to describe to an interviewer in Berlin what he felt constituted the American understanding of the world:

> I mean a sense of identity with destiny that has been born of Protestantism ... [a] belief in the significance and even in the concealed implications of every event. It is precisely the same thing as the much abused doctrines of predestination and inward asceticism. . . . Just think of what it means to every American to believe himself permanently, directly, and responsibly bound to world destiny. . . . It is this magic unity of purpose and change, of destiny and accident, that I have tried to describe.[36]

Jarry can see only the absurdity of the event and the ultimate stupidity of purpose which is completely overcome by chance. *Ubu Roi* is set in Poland, which is to say to the pre-World War I audience that it is nowhere — or anywhere. Poland did not then exist as a political entity. Such a location is within Jarry's view of the universe as absurd and cruel. To emphasize the cruelty, Jarry made the situation the source of comedy. Near the end of the play, for example, someone remarks, thank God for Poland, for if there were no Poland, there would be no Poles. The situation that seemed so intolerable was that there was indeed no Poland, but there were a great many Poles.

Simply, Wilder is more optimistic than the European, although his use of the word *unity* with *purpose* and *chance* implies a balance. In 1954 in a speech before the James Joyce Society, Wilder defended the claims of the individual experience:

> Though I realize that my joy or my grief is but "one" in the ocean of human life, nevertheless it has its reality. I know that the existential thing pouring up in me, my joy or my fear, is a real thing and yet that the intensity with which I feel it can be called absurd. It is absurd to claim that "I," in the vast reaches of time and place and repetition, is worth an assertion.[37]

He continued to explain that a new way was required to place man in an immense field of reference and still dramatize "the validity of the individual as an absolute."[38] Jarry's pessimistic recognition of man's absurd claims was converted by Wilder's extraordinary faith to optimism.

In *The Merchant of Yonkers,* Wilder employed the machinery of farce to effect the ground of timelessness and the absence of a particularized place. Farce is necessarily artificial, and no one need believe in its actuality. Only the truth it presents is important. The characters are stock characters and are not limited by any time. By definition the action of farce is based on an absurd premise, which is, however, developed logically. Having its bases in the imagination, or Human Mind, which ranges with complete freedom, the comic imagination shows us the vast human possibilities that can be ours if only we have the mind and strength to make them so. To be sure, the possibilities are not always pleasant, as for example the plays of Molière. Both the writer and the audience of comedy are in the position of God, for it is they who manipulate, who laugh at, who contain all the actions of the characters moving before them. Jokes and references may be topical, and they may stale with the passage of time; but the action of comedy is timeless because it, like the American, is insubmissive to anything outside it. The comic spirit of *The Merchant of Yonkers* presents the individual existing, related to totality, and freed from obedience to destiny.

Wilder's accomplishment in the willful manipulation of time and space largely went unperceived. Most critics saw *Our Town* as a nostalgic tribute to the good years before World War I in America, carefully limiting its time and place. *The Merchant of Yonkers* was regarded as a failure, having as its only redeeming feature the setting and costumes designed by Boris Aronson. *The Skin of Our Teeth* might have corrected the false view of Wilder's skill, but a large part of its audience felt, or at least proclaimed, that the play was mad and incomprehensible. People by no means ill educated or stupid who saw the original production will claim still, whenever the play is mentioned, that they did not understand a single word of it. Amazingly enough, this attitude is contradicted by those who almost immediately found it simple-minded. In fact, neither attitude is reasonable.

Wilder offered suggestions for staging the play:

At various moments the play superficially resembles other modes, but never thoroughly and never for long: "dream plays"; German expressionism; a comic strip; musical comedy turns. Its prevailing and unifying character is Old Fashioned American Stock Company Theatre.

So the walls are frankly "flats" that ripple when a draft hits them. To be consistent, I should be willing that the Atlantic City boardwalk be one of those vaudeville drops. . . .

A cyclorama has been suggested for the back of the stage; but I have never seen a cyclorama that did not suggest "beauty" of the poetic drama type. I cannot see how background from which the refugees emerge in Act One and the humble not-quite-sublime representatives

of the Philosopher-Hours parade in front of in Act Three could be better represented than by the same brick walls and steam-pipes that were
used in Our Town.

However, while the Antrobuses' sitting-room should have the character of a stage-setting from an old-fashioned stock company play, I do
not mean that it should be dismal or dull.[39]

The "prevailing and unifying character" of the old-fashioned American stock company play was also the manner intended for *The Merchant of Yonkers*. In *The Skin of Our Teeth,* however, it undergoes
a change resulting from the other modes which are superimposed.

When Wilder was at the American Academy in Rome in 1920–
1921, a German had lent him several German expressionist plays by
Georg Kaiser, Fritz von Unruh, Oskar Kokoschka, Walter Hasen-
clever, and Carl Sternheim. Wilder, perhaps too modestly, perhaps
to cross the trail with a red herring, says that he does not remember
them and that his knowledge of German then was not sufficiently
great that he could have got much from them. However, his interest
in expressionist theater techniques was undoubtedly strengthened by
his play-going marathon in Germany in 1928. But most important
to him as lessons was Dreiser's *Plays of the Natural and the Supernatural*. The plays in this peculiar volume exhibit the arbitrarily
arranged reality and dreamlike atmosphere characteristic of expressionism.

The imaginative presentation of human behavior patterns as in a
dream Wilder employed most forcefully at the conclusion of Act II of
The Skin of Our Teeth. The scene is Atlantic City. The characters in
this act come closest to being like the characters in a comic strip. They
are larger than life, and they have a naïve mythic quality. After Antrobus has succumbed to Sabina, after Mrs. Antrobus has tossed into
the sea her letter in which are written "all the things that a woman
knows," after Gladys is exposed in red stockings, and after it is revealed that Henry has again hit a man with a stone, the almost-but-
not-quite-real Atlantic City dissolves. Lights begin to flash and whirl
unpleasantly. A "high whistling noise begins." All the animals are
described as appearing in pairs. Loud thunder is heard. Antrobus tries
in vain to speak to the radio audience. The conveeners snake-dance

across the stage while a voice from the bingo parlor calls the numbers and letters of the game and Esmeralda frighteningly pronounces doom to them all. Throughout, Mrs. Antrobus calls Henry-Cain.

In this mad scene Wilder deserts recognizable reality first of all because such a removal from what is familiar dramatizes best the collapse of the Antrobus world. A realistic scene of destruction could only appear rather mild and perhaps even silly. Secondly, the nightmare on stage, from which the Antrobus family escapes by fleeing through the aisles of the theater, is a representation of the disintegration of man's moral and emotional world. This inner world is mysterious and cannot satisfactorily be represented according to traditional Aristotelian logic. It demands the arbitrary logic of the imagination. The flying scenery, suggested, according to Wilder, by the performances of Olsen and Johnson's *Hellzapoppin'*, is more than comic stage business. The shakiness of the world on stage suggests, even beyond the impermanence of the theatrical representation, the more sinister idea of the impermanence of the particular details of life. Beginning with the fall of Antrobus, or Adam, everything that depended on their faith, the static stability of Eden, is removed and must be recreated.

Mood, so important to the dramaturgy of expressionism, is also used by Wilder, first in *Our Town* and then in *The Skin of Our Teeth*. Near the conclusion of Act II of *Our Town,* many events are viewed as happening simultaneously: first the choir rehearsal with George and Emily talking from their windows across the lawn; then the choir with George talking with his father; finally the ladies returning from choir rehearsal with the speeches of Dr. and Mrs. Gibbs, George and Rebecca, and Mr. Webb and Emily. These events appear slight if they are considered separately, but together they become meaningful, especially after they are summed up in Rebecca's speech about the letter addressed to Jane Crofut. They are given their place in the mind of God. The moonlight, although no attempt is made to reproduce it, is repeatedly described by the characters. This moonlight, which the audience must work to create, combined with the singing of the choir, establishes a mood or feeling which the audience is nearly powerless to resist. Just as with the umbrellas at the funeral in the third act, this mood so prepares the audience for the correct response that the actors must play their parts with the greatest simplicity, keeping limited any display of emotion. If the actors force the scene, it topples into sentimental weeping and reduces the meaning to particularity, although what Wilder has prepared is honest sentiment and a carefully generalized portrayal.

Almost identical effects are created in *The Skin of Our Teeth*. At the conclusion of the first act, to encourage the audience to accept the danger to the entire human group, Wilder has the refugees sing "Jingle Bells" and then "Tenting Tonight." These songs, like the hymns in *Our Town*, are part of the childhood of the audience. The response to the songs, therefore, is automatically an emotional one. The singing colors whatever happens on stage. This primitive emotional reaction is emphasized by the passages in Greek and Hebrew. The foreign words recited dramatically, precisely because the audience do not understand their meaning, touch something in the audience that is deeper than rational argument could go. In a memo, presumably to the director, Elia Kazan, Wilder wrote:

> I earnestly hope you retain the speeches in Greek and Hebrew even if it is bold and may puzzle a portion of the audience, for those who get it, it will be a value so deep-reaching that it will be worth the risk. And I think that with the additional support to the scene of the cold-suspense ... the passage will sustain.[40]

Unfortunately Wilder's plea was not heeded, and the speeches did not appear in the original New York production.

Although both expressionism and Wilder's use of it are based on an ideal vision, expressionism's ideal moves away from ordinary reality and finds its form in situations dependent on the will of the writer. The vision is communicated through what are recognizably artificial situations. Wilder is equally artificial, but most prominently in the area of his stagecraft. By eliminating clichés of staging, he is able to offer the clichés of life as one kind of truth. He learned technique from expressionism, but ultimately he rejected expressionism's vision of the world as being too specialized.

In his major plays Wilder has consistently sought to emphasize those aspects of the stage involved in pretense. The success of such pretense is peculiar to the theater because of the audience. Sabina, who has protested that she had been unable to understand a single word of *The Skin of Our Teeth,* wonderingly confesses in the first act, "Now that you audience are listening to this, too, I understand it a little better."[41] He has returned theatrical conventions to their rightful position in order to emphasize the idea of imitation and to capture "not verisimilitude but reality."[42] This reality, whose time is always *now* and whose place is always *here,* clarifies and enlarges the endless repetition of human experience. More important, it provides a way to explain the peculiar life of twentieth-century people.

IV

CHARACTERIZATION AND NARRATION

---

*The dramatist's principal interest being the movement
of the story, he is willing to resign the more detailed
aspects of characterization to the actor and is often
rewarded beyond his expectation.*

CHARACTERIZATION and narration, in Thornton Wilder's theater, are inextricably bound. The two are related not merely as a matter of being consistent to a single style; their unity and Wilder's use of
it determine the style, for his practice is to give over psychological
characterization in favor of an arbitrary and artificial arrangement of
events.

In "Some Thoughts on Playwriting" Wilder defined his goals in
characterization.

> Imaginative narration — the invention of souls and destinies — is to
> a philosopher an all but indefensible activity.
>
> Its justification lies in the fact that the communication of ideas from
> one mind to another inevitably reaches the point where exposition
> passes into illustration, into parable, metaphor, allegory, and myth.[1]

Characters, therefore, are created to convey ideas, and they will naturally make their appearance as symbols.

Gertrude Stein in *Narration,* for which Wilder wrote the introduction, explained how the arbitrary, imaginative creation of characters
was superior to relying on the facts.

> Vasari and Plutarch are like that, they make them up so completely that
> if they are not invented, they might as well be they do not really feel that

any of the ones about whom they tell had any life except the life they are given by their telling. That can happen and when it does it is writing.[2]

Wilder converted this idea of Gertrude Stein's, that the characters are more real when they are imagined, from narrative prose to theatrical writing; he left the characterization so general that the people in his plays must really be created in the imagination of the audience, although, of course, the play contains characters, and actors must play them.

The first manuscript version of *Our Town* is particularly emphatic in its special treatment of characterization. The Stage Manager played all the children but Emily and George. In addition, he played Simon Stimson and, as in the final version, Mrs. Forrest and Mr. Morgan, the druggist, as well as the minister who marries George and Emily. The audience was required in this version to imagine not merely the particulars of characters but also their very presence. Wilder felt it necessary at least once to tell the audience what he was doing. The Stage Manager says, "Now I'm Mr. Morgan in front of his drugstore." This was later removed, and the Stage Manager simply took the speeches of Mrs. Forrest and Mr. Morgan without any fuss, and the roles of Stimson, Rebecca, and Wally were given to actors.

Wilder depends very heavily on his audience for much of the work that has been traditionally expected from the playwright himself, but he derives advantages from this kind of writing. In one of the letters to Sol Lesser, who produced the filming of *Our Town,* concerning whether or not Emily should die, Wilder distinguished between the stage and the film.

> In a movie you see the people so *close to* that a different relation was established. In a theatre they are halfway abstractions in an allegory; in a movie they are very concrete. So insofar as it's a concrete happening, it's not important that she die; it's even disproportionately cruel that she die.[3]

This short comment reveals much about Wilder's concept of his own work. First, he views *Our Town* as an allegory, probably as something like a twentieth-century *Everyman*. One of the important qualities of allegory is that characterization is absent, except when it serves to distinguish abstract qualities, such as hate or lust. Wilder recognizes that his own characters fit the situation of allegory in that they are "halfway abstractions." Emily and George represent, only as much as it is absolutely necessary, two individuals. Their chief function is to be a young girl and a young boy.

This kind of characterization determines what happens on stage. It is the reason why a complete marriage proposal is not presented. Emily and George do not have personalities sufficiently distinct to participate in so individual a procedure. When anybody marries, his wedding is much like that of anybody else. Anybody's *deciding* to marry and *proposing* is one and one and one. Each proposal is different from the rest, and most frequently, as a result, marriage proposals are an event for comic dramatization.

The wedding ceremony is a thing altogether different. The occasion itself, the ceremony, like the occasion of the birthday in Act III, carries with it advantages to Wilder's allegory. First, both are the kind of event about which everybody has a ready-made memory. Secondly, the witnesses of such events are called together without any particularization. Wedding guests behave pretty much the same at one wedding as at another. People weep at weddings; they are happy at birthdays. Each celebration comes equipped with a behavior pattern which is available to the entire audience, and it is independent of George and Emily.

Wilder has not offered simply a wedding. In the real world most people require some personal interest in the bride or groom to make their wedding interesting. In the theater a different situation exists. Again in a letter to Lesser, Wilder wrote:

> My only worry is that — realistically done — your wedding scene won't be interesting enough, and that it will reduce many of the surrounding scenes to ordinaryness. . . .
> On the stage with *Our Town* the novelty was supplied by
> (1) economy of effect in scenery.
> (2) the minister was played by the Stage Manager.
> (3) the thinking-aloud passages.
> (4) the oddity of hearing Mrs. Soames' gabble during the ceremony.

(5) the young people's moments of alarm....

— And for a story that is so generalized [the danger of dwindling to the conventional] ... is great.

The play interested because every few minutes there was a new bold effect in presentation-methods....

I know you'll realize that I don't mean boldness or oddity for their own sakes, but merely as the almost indispensible reinforcement and refreshment of a play that was never intended to be interesting for its story alone, or even for its background.[4]

Wilder knew that neither the plot nor the *mise en scène* was intended to be interesting. This is a partial answer for those people who were enchanted by the story of a typical New England town. Also the wedding of an Emily Webb and a George Gibbs is scarcely the point, for the wedding is everybody's. The unusual staging retained the interest in an event which takes place essentially with people who are not people at all, but ideas.

One of Lesser's letters to Wilder illustrates what might happen to *Our Town* if insistence on detail and private motive were applied.

It has been suggested for movie purposes a means to be found to attach the third act to circumstances already within the play.... By this it is meant that perhaps there should be a problem affecting the married life of Emily and George growing out of the differences in their mentalities. I cite the following only as an example: —

Emily is brighter than George; in her youth she has the best memory in her class — she recites like "silk off a spool" — she helps George in his mathematics — she is articulate — George is not — she is "going to make speeches all the rest of her life." ...

Query: Could it be Emily's subtlety in the soda-fountain scene that causes George to make the decision not to go to Agricultural School? The audience gets this, but George feels it is his own voluntary thought. He makes the decision not to go.

Could Emily, after death, re-visit her fifth wedding anniversary ... and now see her mistake?

Emily in life is likely to have been overambitious for George, wanting him to accomplish all the things he would have known had he gone to Agricultural School, but which he has had to learn mainly by experience. In a single sentence we could establish that George did not de-

velop the farm as efficiently and as rapidly as Emily thought he should
have. She continued to get ideas out of newspapers and books, as she
did out of her school books, and had tried to explain them to George,
but he was slow in grasping them. She had been impatient very often.
Someone else's farm may have been progressing faster than George's
and she may not have liked that. . . .

Now she sees this. She remembers she was responsible for his not going to Agricultural School. She has overlooked many of George's virtues — she took them all for granted. All this was her mistake. . . .

Could there be a great desire to live, to profit by what she has just
seen, rather than go back to the grave — should she long to live —
would the audience, witnessing this picture, pull for her to live — and
she does?

. . . It would only change the expression of your philosophy, not the
philosophy itself, which would be retained.[5]

Lesser's suggestions indicate that he lacked any real understanding of
the play. His final comment — "it would only change the expression of
your philosophy" — suggests that he does not understand any plays at
all. His emphasis is on event for its own sake, and his plan is rather
like the scenario for a soap opera.

Wilder answered Lesser with restraint, but firmly:

I feel pretty concrete about trying to dissuade you against showing Emily returning to her fifth wedding anniversary and regretting that she
had been an unwise wife.

(1) It throws out the window the return to the 12th birthday which
you feel is sufficient [*sic?* insufficiently] tied up with the earlier part
of the picture, but which is certain of its effect.

(2) It introduces a lot of plot preparation in the earlier part of the
picture that would certainly be worse than what's there now. Scene of
George running the farm incompetently. Scene of Emily upbraiding
him.

(3) It makes Emily into a school-marm "improving" superior person. The traits that you point out *are* in her character . . . but I put them
there to prevent her being pure-village-girl-sweet-ingenue. But push
them a few inches further and she becomes priggish.

(4) The balance of the play, reposing between vast stretches of time
and suggestions of generalized multitudes of people requires that the

fathers and mothers, and especially the hero and heroine, be pretty near the norm of everybody, every boy and every girl.

If this is made into an ineffectual-but-good-hearted-husband and superior-interfering-wife, the balance is broken.

It's not so much new "plotting" that is needed, as it is refreshing detail-play over the simple but sufficient plot that's there.[6]

George and Emily, individually psychologized and motivated, would tumble into another one of those hopelessly stupid stories of boy and girl, and a dull one at that.

Successful though it was, *Our Town* could not be endlessly imitated. It was necessary to adapt to other kinds of plays the lessons Wilder had learned. His very next play was the farce *The Merchant of Yonkers,* superficially a change from *Our Town;* yet the attitude toward characterization in both plays is similar.

In a note of a letter written to Max Reinhardt, who directed the play, Wilder described in part his own concept of it: "the image of simple & direct farce with emphasis on character work and the personal relations of player to player here submerged under stylized treatment of the whole."[7] At about the time of the opening of his play, he theorized about the nature of farce.

The pleasures of farce, like those of the detective story, are those of development, pattern and logic.

A "pure" farce would be all pattern and would admit no mixture. Comedy, which is the clarification of unsocial human traits through exaggeration, may benefit by a dash of farce, especially toward the close of the evening, but farce dare not lean too far toward the exposition of character.[8]

He desired to use stock characters, eliminating the development of character and, as in *Our Town,* expressing only as much personality as was needed to define their enduring types as miser, fool, widow, and so on.

However, Wilder, knowing his American audience, recognized that "pure" farce, which flourished with ease only in the theaters of Spain or France, would not work. Also he required that the individual make itself felt within the type. Having no tradition to fall back on, he tempered the "pure" farce.

Perhaps — as with the "pure" detective story — it would not be so desirable after all. Perhaps a wavering among other elements makes it bearable: toward humor its natural enemy, for humor is the acknowledgment of one's kinship with frailty; toward character drawing; toward picturesqueness, a static quality; even toward pathos — perhaps all these are necessary to keep it from the empty triumph of its two fundamental drives: logic and objectivity.[9]

The two major characters, Mrs. Levi and Vandergelder, illuminate Wilder's meaning and show how he wavered among the other elements, especially humor, character drawing, and pathos. Mrs. Levi strayed into *The Merchant of Yonkers* from Molière's *L'Avare*, which in turn is based in part on the *Aulularia* of Plautus.

L'Avare is close to being a "pure" farce, if the term has any meaning. A comparison of Wilder's adaptation with Molière's original demonstrates the debt Wilder owes.[10] *The Merchant of Yonkers*, however, is very different from the usual farce. It adopts a more kindly and gentle attitude toward the human faults and failings of the characters. No question ever arises about the intent of Molière's Frosine and Harpagon. Frosine brilliantly and ruthlessly is after as much of Harpagon's money as she can get. She will cheat and lie to secure her ends. Harpagon equally cleverly fights to hand over as little of his cash as he may. Taken without the laughter, the human behavior displayed in the scene between Frosine and Harpagon is stripped of the hypocrisy that makes it bearable in real life. The two make a frightening pair. When the play ends with the lovers uniting, there is the horrifying vision of Harpagon returning to his own beloved, money: "Et moi, voir ma chère cassette."[11] Such a vision of the human animal is almost too appalling to accept, but Molière, in displaying so limited a view of human motives, pitting Frosine's cupidity against Harpagon's, has exaggerated it absurdly — though logically — to the degree that we can laugh at it as we recognize its truth.

Dolly Levi and Vandergelder are like innocent children when compared with Molière's characters. Vandergelder, it is true, is a miser, but the audience knows from his soliloquy that chinks exist in the armor of his greed. He is willing to risk money for adventure. Harpagon's money is his adventure. Mrs. Levi's financial theories are as simple as Frosine's, but they are more humane. "Pardon my expression: money's like manure, which isn't worth anything until it's spread about encouraging young things to grow."[12] Mrs. Levi has taken for her own Francis Bacon's "Money is like muck, not good except it be spread."[13] In the light of their own words, the struggle between Mrs. Levi and Horace Vandergelder cannot be understood, as it can with Frosine and Harpagon, as the attempt by two clever people to outwit each other. Mrs. Levi is going to marry Vandergelder to save him from his money, to return him to the human race. She is a delightful busybody, and she will reveal Vandergelder to be basically a goodhearted man. Frosine does not consider Harpagon as a person at all.

As Wilder adapted Molière, he changed some detail to suit his own characters. He added the subplot of Mrs. Molloy, which has no equivalent in Molière's play. Molière's unpleasant satire, at the expense of both youth and age, with its nasty physical detail, was inappropriate to *The Merchant of Yonkers,* and it has been softened and removed in time. This is the static picturesque of which Wilder wrote and whose effect is nostalgic, preventing satire. Molière's brilliant catalogue of the girl's dowry, the list of her frugal ways, is an inverse list of contemporary follies; the same list is only humorous in Mrs. Levi's speech. Molière has skillfully employed every speech as a weapon in his attack on society; Wilder merely reveals Mrs. Levi's preposterous ingenuity.

Where it was useful Wilder employed the type characters from farce without any tempering. The play warns against the difficulties of achieving the dream situation of "all the good things a poor person has, and, all the good meals a rich person has,"[14] but it demonstrates just as positively that it is not impossible for the individual to break out of the pattern established by farce.

Like Sabina in *The Skin of Our Teeth,* Wilder does not "think the theatre is a place where people's feelings ought to be hurt."[15] It is not that he is hiding his head in the sand away from the horror of ordinary living or the peculiar dreariness of the twentieth-century world. Mrs. Levi says, "It's nice people, also, who tear their fellow men to pieces."[16] His characterization hopes to celebrate man's positive possibilities, however remote, for Mrs. Levi concludes with the great American wish: "Oh, my friends, — fellow fools, fellow monsters, — I want to live in a world where there is just enough money for us to enjoy ourselves in moderation, and just enough freedom for us to play the fool in moderation."[17]

Characterization in *The Skin of Our Teeth* and *The Alcestiad* are further developments of the idea of stage character Wilder had already used. *The Skin of Our Teeth* updated the "half-abstractions in an allegory" from *Our Town*. The family name Antrobus is really the Greek word *anthropos,* human being or man, thinly disguised, and the family is back-dated to the beginnings of man also, as the newscaster at the beginning of the play announces about the objects found in the theater by the cleaning women: "Among these objects found today was a wedding ring, inscribed: To Eva from Adam. Genesis II:18."[18] The Antrobus family is really the same as the Gibbses and the Webbs under its mid-twentieth-century suburban exterior. Conventions at Atlantic City, the A & P, and the movies appear in place of milk delivery by horse and wagon, the country drugstore, and the wood-burning stove, but the particularizing details are unimportant. The abstract idea of family is pictured in both.

Sabina in particular brings to *The Skin of Our Teeth* the spirit of farce. Her character design moves, sometimes rather violently, between the allegorical temptress and the standard farcical maid, although neither element is ever really absent from the other. They are pictured as varieties of the same personality. In a letter from Tallulah Bankhead, who was the first Sabina, to Michael Meyerberg she quoted from Wilder:

> It's so necessary for the play that each of your changes of mood and especially the "break-throughs" to the audience come through with such spontaneous inner reality that they don't seem to the audience to be author's contrivances but pure *SABINA NATURE.*[19]

The Alcestiad posed a problem slightly different from those of any of the early plays. Alcestis was not simply an American housewife and mother like Mrs. Webb or Mrs. Antrobus, although she could not be foreign to that ideal. She had to be something more. Oddly Wilder achieved his end by making her something less. Alcestis has no peculiarities of character whatever. Her personality is important only as she illustrates intensity of existence. She is pure allegory. It is as though Wilder had reduced all his earlier characterization to its essence and molded it to resemble the form of a woman. Because, however, her characterization is not naïve and because she is provided with details of living — a father, a husband, children — Alcestis does not emerge in the play as uninteresting as most allegorical figures. Strangely, she seems in possession of an existence that is clearer and closer to the basis of life than most imagined characters. At the same time, as the play moves toward its conclusion and Alcestis emerges more and more as a symbol, one loses real interest in her fate as an individual. This loss of interest, too, is set to work by Wilder. Since the play is without tragic vision, the loss of interest in Alcestis' particular fate, except as it illuminates the fate of millions, prevents all personal anguish and grief. The audience are left only with the idea.

In transposing his myth to a modern play, Wilder does not use to any great degree the familiar device of ironically posing his characters against their counterparts in classical literature. The two exceptions are Tiresias and Hercules.

Tiresias is a comic character. He enters with the boy who guides him.

(*Surprisingly loud*): Is this the palace of Midas, King of Crete? (*The Boy starts pulling his sleeve and whispering into his ear.*) I mean is this the palace of Oedipus, King of Thebes? (*Striking the boy with his stick.*) Stop pulling at me and buzzing. I know what I'm saying, — bees, wasps, and hornets! . . . Silence and hold your tongues: Zeus, father of Gods and men, has commanded . . . has commanded . . . Boy, what has he commanded? (Boy *whispers. Tiresias strikes him.*) Well, you don't have to run on . . . has commanded that Apollo, my master, — that Apollo come down from Olympus; and that he live on earth for one year . . . solstice to solstice . . . live as a man among men. I have given my message. — Boy lead me to the road.[20]

This Tiresias is an ill-tempered old man who forgets his messages and where they ought to be delivered. Had Wilder presented a Tiresias like that of Sophocles, the characterization would have been grotesquely and inadvertently comic, for who today can believe, without the distance time provides, in Tiresias? The calculated comedy eliminates any falseness in Tiresias, and at the same time it permits his messages from the gods to be utterly arbitrary and, therefore, frightening and mysterious. And since Tiresias is a typical, grumbling old man, all need for psychology and private motive is cut off.

Hercules is, at first, like his counterpart in Euripides' *Alcestis*, a moderately loud, cheerful athletic cliché who, if he does have any peculiar psychology, keeps it hidden from sight by a series of well-worn jokes, by a naïve attitude (whether deliberate or not), and by a dependence on physical acts rather than intellectual distinctions. He is also a hero with a long and noble tradition from Euripides, through the Stoics, Seneca in particular, to the Renaissance. Wilder's hero changes from a mildly comic boob to the embodiment of a position in a scale of philosophical values, and this second characterization is much like the one in Euripides' *Heracles*. William Arrowsmith, writing of the Euripidean play, observed:

> In the shaping of the characters, in their attributes and motives, in the theology and received values to which the action appeals, convention is everywhere visible. Character is essentially static, the action as a whole leached of any really tragic movement. All the emotional stops of a melodramatic situation have been pulled: we move from the despair of the helpless family to the sudden coming of the savior hero to the triumphant final diapason of vindicated divine justice. The characters are only lightly dubbed in, certainly no more so than is necessary to maintain the illusion that these are real people in a situation of unqualified peril.[21]

Unmodified, this applies also to Wilder's play in its structure and characterization. The purity and simplicity of Euripides have been set to work, making a different world view.

Obviously Wilder's plays depend heavily on the quality and kind of acting they receive. One of the most difficult tasks Wilder set for the actor was the pantomime in *Our Town*. This movement without props has frequently been compared with Chinese theater, and that relationship seemed all the more probable in the light of his two stays in China as a child when his father was Consul General, first at Hong Kong and then at Shanghai. He has never seen a full-length Chinese play, however, and he did not see *The Yellow Jacket* by George C. Hazleton and Benrimo either, with which *Our Town* is sometimes identified, though he did, as he has said, "read all about it."

In 1930 Mei Lan-fang, the great Chinese actor, and certainly one of the great actors of any style, played in New York. His success, both on the stage and in the drawing room, was astounding. That an art form as foreign as Chinese play acting should triumph on Broadway is surprising, if also gratifying; that Mei Lan-fang should have become overwhelmingly fashionable in society is more to be expected and less agreeable. Tickets were virtually unobtainable. Fortunately Wilder, as someone's guest, saw one of Mei Lan-fang's extraordinary performances. It is difficult, if not impossible, to assess accurately the impact and value of an action which is in the past, never to be repeated, and which one has never seen. Still something must be said about Mei Lan-fang because of his effect on Wilder.

In his review in the *New Republic,* Stark Young wrote of the unfamiliar conventions of Chinese art.

> When purely symbolistic, these conventions represent — without reproducing — ideas, actions, things, exactly as words do, which in themselves are nothing but sound. There is this difference, however, between these symbols and words: a movement or object symbolizing a beautiful idea, personage, place, tends to be created into something in itself more beautiful and worthy of the association, whereas a word remains the same, plus perhaps our efforts to put beauty into its employment. These conventions in themselves have doubtless, therefore, taken on a greater and greater perfection.[22]

Stark Young's explanation of the symbolistic aspect of Mei Lan-fang's beauty helps to explain the pantomime in Wilder's staging. In *Our Town* it was used mainly to express the chores about the home: preparing meals, stringing beans, mowing the grass, delivering the paper and milk — activities that are repeated either daily or seasonally.

In the New York *Times* in 1938 Wilder wrote:

> The theatre longs to represent the symbols of things, not the things themselves. All the lies it tells . . . all those lies enhance the one truth that is there — the truth that dictated the story, the myth.[23]

To reproduce the acts in words, to tell about them, is totally unsatisfactory to the stage, simply because it is not dramatic. To reproduce the acts exactly, with a real stove or a real lawn mower, is to subtract from them their symbolistic implications: the idea of repetition, the idea that they "represent — without reproducing — " an important part of living, and the idea that they convey something more enduring than the actual act itself. Not merely the convention of pantomime but also what the pantomime presents takes on a "greater and greater perfection" and thereby enhances the myth.

Stark Young continued:

> What we must say about the realism and abstraction and stylization of Mei Lan-fang's art is that, exactly as is the case in the classic Chinese art, we are astonished at the precision of its realistic notations and renderings, and are dazzled by the place these take in the highly stylized and removed whole that the work of art becomes. . . . none of these is impersonation or reality in the usual sense. They are real only in the sense that great sculptures or paintings are real, through their motion in repose, their impression of shock, brief duration and beautiful finality. Every now and then — very rarely — in acting we see this happen: I mean a final quality in some emotion, the presentation of that truth which confirms and enlarges our sense of reality.[24]

As Stark Young suggests, one of the distinctive advantages of those conventions of the theater closest to the roots of drama is that they are stylized, yet recognizable; they represent the essence of the idea, the action, or the emotion. They are the barest bones of eternal truth raised to a level that all may recognize. At the same time, when any individual actor of some stature interprets the conventions, they become particularized without losing any of their possibilities as enduring modes of behavior. On his bare stage Wilder sought to dramatize this balance between the individual and the many. The pantomime in his early successful plays results from his attempts to return the imagination to drama and to restore vitality to its essential make-believe. He wrote in "Some Thoughts on Playwriting": "The stage is fundamental pretense and it thrives on the acceptance of that fact and in the multiplication of additional pretenses."[25] The dreary realism of early twentieth-century theater along with the fantastic realism of the cinema seemed to militate against the frank use of pretense in drama. In contrast, Wilder, borrowing from a foreign tradition, self-consciously focused on stage conventions.

His interest in pantomime was reinforced by the work of Richard Boleslavsky, who produced Wilder's first play, *The Trumpet Shall Sound,* and whose work Wilder greatly admired. Boleslavsky was trained at the Moscow Art Theater when it was most flourishing during the prerevolutionary time, and his theories of acting are based on that tradition. In his book *Acting, The First Six Lessons,* he explains a method of training actors based on a German kindergarten game called *Achtungspiele.* Boleslavsky's students were not permitted to tell what they had observed in themselves or in others, but had to act it out without the aid of any properties. Like the characters in *Our Town,* the students were all busily performing and repeating everyday activities silently. There are many virtues in this activity, but two of them in relation to Wilder's work stand out. It makes the actor "sensitive to sincerity and make-believe. . . . And lastly, . . . it enriches his inner life by full and extensive consumption of everything in outward life."[26] Boleslavsky's sincerity is the "realer" thing that Wilder finds in patently artificial theatrical techniques; the actor's make-believe has no support other than that which he can provide for himself. The last reward, enriching the inner life, is another way of expressing Stark Young's observation that Mei Lan-fang superimposed realistic detail upon his very stylized and rigidly controlled acting. Wilder demands from the actors of his early one-act plays and of *Our Town* that they attempt something like Mei Lan-fang's expression of a reality above the casual and a permanence beyond the brevity of each performance.

But as Arrowsmith said of Euripides' *Heracles,* the "characters are only lightly dubbed in." Wilder, concerned with just this matter, wrote in "Some Thoughts on Playwriting": "Characterization in a play is like a blank check which the dramatist accords to the actor for him to fill in."[27] This idea is presented in a more expanded form in the chapter on characterization in Richard Boleslavsky's book *Acting.* He makes an interesting distinction between the mind of the author and the emotions of the characters portrayed. It is a mistake, he says, to imagine the way the character would think. "The most powerful weapon of an author is his mind. The quality of it, the speed, depth, alertness, brilliance."[28] All the actor has to do "is grasp the characterization of . . . the author's mind and follow it."[29] About the rules of characterization governing the emotions of a character, Boleslavsky protests:

> The emotion of a character is the only sphere where the author should pay attention to the actor's demands and adjust his writings to the actor's interpretation. Or, an actor is justified in adjusting the author's writing to achieve the best results for his own emotional outlines of the part.[30]

The distinctions Boleslavsky draws between the mind of the author and the emotions of the character are another way of distinguishing between Gertrude Stein's Human Nature and the Human Mind or Wilder's idea of the many and the individual. Wilder is aware that the characters in his plays are created anew by each different actor; in fact, he depends on it, for he has left the material with which the actor will work very general. A good actor brings the idea to life. Whether the actor is good or bad, however, the meaning of the plays will manifest itself in performance, because Wilder has carefully calculated the movement of his story. The narration concerns itself with the Human Mind.

He wrote in "Some Thoughts on Playwriting":

> The dramatist through working in the theater gradually learns not merely to take account of the presence of the collaborators, but to derive advantage from them; and he learns, above all, to organize the play in such a way that its strength lies not in appearances beyond his control, but in the succession of events and in the unfolding of an idea, in narration.[31]

He added:

> The theater carries the art of narration to a higher power than the novel or the epic poem. The theater is unfolding action and in the disposition of events the author may exercise a governance so complete that the distortions effected by the physical appearance of the actors, by the fancies of scene painters and the misunderstandings of directors, fall into relative insignificance. It is just because the theater is an art of many col-

laborators, with the constant danger of grave misinterpretation, that the dramatist learns to turn his attention to the laws of narration, its logic and its deep necessity of presenting a unifying idea stronger than its mere collection of happenings. The dramatist must be by instinct a story teller.[32]

The importance of the story that is told is not, however, the sequence of events so much as the arrangement of the sequence. What Wilder means is that the events or the happenings have become unimportant in themselves. An event does not possess meaning simply because it happened as it might have in the past.

Wilder wrote, again in "Some Thoughts on Playwriting," that story telling

> springs, not, as some have said, from an aversion of general ideas, but from instinctive coupling of idea and illustration. . . . The myth, the parable, the fable are the fountain-head of all fiction, and in them is seen most clearly the didactic, moralizing employment of a story.[33]

The plot must have a significance beyond the events recounted, whose real function is to illustrate an idea. Wilder wrote of the "laws of narration," without saying what they are, although he had mentioned the eternal present and forward movement. In order to understand more what Wilder means by these terms in relation to the "laws of narration," we need look no further than Gertrude Stein's *Narration*. In considering the arrangement in narrative, she wrote:

> Narrative has been the telling of anything because there has been always has been a feeling that something followed another thing that there was succession in happening.
>
> In a kind of way what has made the Old Testament such permanently good reading is that really in a way in the Old Testament writing there really was not any such thing there was not really any succession of anything and really in the Old Testament there is really no sentence existing and no paragraphing. . . . So then in the Old Testament writing there is really no actual conclusion that anything is progressing that one thing is succeeding another thing, that anything in that sense in the sense of succeeding happening is a narrative of anything, but most writing is based on this thing most writing has been a

real narrative writing a telling of the story of anything in the way that thing has been happening and now everything is not that thing there is at present not a sense of anything being successively happening, moving is in every direction beginning and ending is not really exciting, anything is anything, any thing is happening and anybody can know anything at any time that anything is happening and so really and truly is there any sentence and any paragraphing is there prose and poetry as the same or different things is there now any narrative of any successive thing.[34]

To explain what she meant, she wrote further:

> When I first began writing really just began writing, I was tremendously impressed by anything by everything having a beginning and a middle and an ending ... but then gradually well if you are an American gradually you find that really it is not necessary not really necessary that anything that everything has a beginning and a middle and an ending and so you struggling with anything as anything has begun and began does not really mean that thing does not really mean beginning or begun. ....
>
> And it was right and quite a natural thing that the book I wrote in which I was escaping from the inevitable narrative of anything of everything succeeding something of needing to be succeeding that is following anything of anything of everything consisting that is the emotional and the actual value of anything counting in anything having beginning and middle and ending it was natural that the book I wrote in which I was escaping from all this inevitably in narrative writing I should have called The Making of Americans.[35]

"Beginning and ending is not really exciting," she says. "Moving is in every direction." Gertrude Stein has associated this moving in every direction, the absence of a beginning and a middle and an end, with America. This association proved especially useful to Wilder. The difficult problem of how to end the play, which was never successfully solved in *The Trumpet Shall Sound,* does not exist, because there is no resolution. Time continues, and all answers, therefore, are left behind imbedded in time past. Answers appeal only to Human Nature, which counts for less than the Human Mind. The problem becomes one of imaginative narration. Wilder told the *Paris Review:* "It lies in the effort to employ the past tense in such a way that it does not rob those events of their character of having occurred in freedom."[36]

Gertrude Stein's conclusions about writing showed Wilder how to organize his plays so that his central idea would manifest itself beyond any aberrations of his collaborators. He learned to present a unified idea in a succession of events, and he learned to create the events so that they would never assume any importance, because they were never permitted either to be interesting or to reach a climax. The characters in the events never knew what was going to happen next, because nothing ever happened. Wilder's audience may never remember that Mrs. Gibbs and Mrs. Webb were stringing beans in the first act of *Our Town*, but they will have kept in mind that mothers always provide for their families. The nearest to a conclusion which the play is permitted to reach is the wedding, and a wedding is as much a beginning as an ending.

Gertrude Stein's idea of narration is responsible for the presentation in *Our Town* of a series of small glimpses of life, each without beginning or ending. This technique required the character of the Stage Manager, so that some continuity was kept between each event and the next. In *The Matchmaker*, Wilder used the direct address to audience in the four major soliloquies; in *The Skin of Our Teeth*, Sabina; and in *The Alcestiad*, Apollo and Death. In an interview with the *Saturday Review of Literature* after the opening of *Our Town*, Wilder said: "In an age in which an audience contains such varying approaches to fundamental questions of life a commentator is useful for delivering signposts."[37] It is the varying approaches of the audience, the absence of a point of view in the modern world, especially in America, that persuaded Gertrude Stein that "there is at present not a sense of anything being successively happening." That she should cite the Old Testament as a kind of writing "without really any succession of anything" is particularly interesting. The temporal or geographical locations have no significance except in their relation to God. This presentness was perfectly possible in the Old Testament because of the claim to absolute authority which it possessed. Since it is impossible today to claim absolute authority or to invoke the will of God as a motivating force, Wilder found it necessary to place the Stage Manager in control of his imaginary world in order to guide the audience. He does not instruct the audience what to think, but like all well-integrated characters in a play, he guides that audience into understanding what the action presented on the stage represents. The Stage Manager, through his authority, combines Wilder's concepts of Characterization and Narration.

V

AN AMERICAN LANGUAGE

---

*Language for ... [the writer] is the instrument for
digesting experience, for explaining himself to himself.*

WHERE the language is inadequate, the play is unsatisfactory. Any
evaluation of the plays of the past would accept such an axiom without
serious reservation. Our own American theater, on the other hand, is
not recognized by a skillful manipulation of language. In fact the writing of Eugene O'Neill, who is regarded by some as the great American
playwright, is generally if impatiently conceded to be simply bad.
Good writing, when it is not the object of outright contempt, is largely
an irrelevant factor on the American stage; to complete the dismal
picture, actors frequently take their revenge by speaking badly. In
contrast and not necessarily always to his benefit, Wilder has consistently maintained a concern for the theoretical as well as the practical
possibilities of language. Not only has he always written with extraordinary care and precision but he has also thoughtfully considered the
function of language, what it could do and, more important, what it
could not do. Perhaps this is so because Wilder's writing ranges beyond the walls of the theater, and American novelists and poets especially have demonstrated a concern, an obsession almost, with language.

Wilder's early career marks his struggle to learn a difficult but important lesson: that writing is something more than beautiful sen-
tences. In the preface to *The Angel That Troubled the Waters* in 1928,
Wilder connected beauty with language, especially in their didactic
functions. Regretting the overwhelming vulgarization of language, he

wrote, "It is too late to arrest the deterioration of our greatest English words."[1] Furthermore, he associated language with religion:

> All that is fairest in the Christian tradition [is] made repugnant to the new generations by reason of the diction in which it is expressed. The intermittent sincerity of generations of clergymen and teachers have [*sic*] rendered embarrassing and even ridiculous all the terms of the spiritual life. . . . The revival of religion is almost a matter of rhetoric.[2]

He said also that "beyond logic, beauty is the only persuasion."[3] This connection of language and religion and beauty is a hang-over from the late nineteenth-century aesthetics conceived, for example, by Walter Pater, where religion finds its most complete expression in beauty. It is, of course, ultimately based on the Romantic conception of art or beauty, which held that the beautiful, natural or otherwise, in stirring men's minds achieved, or should achieve, some far-reaching moral effect. If a fellow American, Ezra Pound, in 1920 in *Hugh Selwyn Mauberley* could bathe the pre-Raphaelite period and the nineties in an ironic light, it is still not unreasonable that a young man even eight years later introducing works, most of which he had written before, during, and shortly after World War I as an undergraduate, could speak of beauty's persuasion. Wilder's introduction to Pater's "tide of honeyed words" and the intimate relationship between religion and art was through George Moore's early novels, which Wilder admired extravagantly even during his Oberlin days and whose language he unhappily attempted to imitate. Much later when he had outgrown Moore's literary influence Wilder was to meet him, neglected by the literary world but still playing the *enfant terrible,* at Lady Cunard's in London. But when he began writing, Wilder concentrated less on the work to be made than on capturing beauty, forgetting, as Jacques Maritain puts it, that beauty is more than the "operational end — being the end beyond the end."[4] This accounts in part for the preciosity of the Three Minute Plays and the self-consciously beautiful writing in the first three novels. The writing deceives the reader and certainly deceived Wilder into believing that the subject matter, with its retreat from the vulgarity of the actual world for one of beauty, was more substantial than it really is.

Gertrude Stein, describing her own temptations by beautiful language and the resulting intoxication, warned Wilder that it was always preferable, if not an absolute necessity, to be sober. "Melody," she wrote, "should always be a by-product it should never be an end in itself it should not be a thing by which you live if you really and truly are one who is to do anything."[5] As Wilder has made abundantly clear in his later writing about language, his own awakening from the nineteenth century and its definition of beauty (Melody) resulted from what Gertrude Stein taught him about being an American, in time, in space, and in religion.

In his essay "Toward an American Language," Wilder observed:

> The English language was molded to express the English experience of life. . . . That achievement went hand in hand with the comparable achievement of forging the language which conveyed so accurately their senses of space, time, and identity. Those senses are not ours and the American people and American writers have long been engaged in reshaping the inherited language to express modes of apprehension.[6]

For Gertrude Stein the difference between the English experience and the American is first of all one of geography and how geography determines life. "In England," she wrote,

> the daily island life was the daily life and it was solidly that daily life. . . . They relied on it so completely that they did not describe it they just had it and told it. . . .
> In America . . . the daily everything was not the daily living and generally speaking there is not a daily everything. They do not have the daily living and so they do not have this as something they are telling.[7]

In America, with its boundless space, a peculiar kind of movement or energy was substituted for the enclosed daily living of the English islanders.

> Think of anything, of cowboys, of movies, of detective stories, of anybody who goes anywhere or stays at home and is an American and you will realize that it is something strictly American to conceive a space that is filled with moving, a space of time that is filled always filled with moving.[8]

And this movement or energy with which the American fills his spaces of — significantly — time is not to be confused with motion. Gertrude Stein explained that the motor of a car can go whether or not the car is being propelled forward. To tell her readers about the going of the motor without bothering about the irrelevant motion of the car was the problem she set herself.

> And if I could in any way and I have done it in every way if I could make a portrait of that inside them without any description of what they are doing and what they are saying then I too was neither repeating, nor remembering nor being in a confusion.[9]

The confusion she wished to avoid in repeating and remembering was both the already known and comprehended experience of the past embodied in language and a fixed or static daily living expressed in language that was without moving. How was the American writer to make the English language move?

The first arrivals in America, according to Wilder, all had one thing in common.

> Their sense of identity did not derive from their relation to their environment. The meaning which their lives had for them was inner and individual....
>
> Independence is momentum....
>
> Separatism is a momentum.[10]

This separation which is a kind of moving is, said Gertrude Stein, fundamental to all American writing, "a separation from what is chosen to what is that from which it has been chosen."[11] To demonstrate what she meant, she observed about Henry James that he

> needed the paragraph because he too was just there, but, and this is the thing to notice, his whole paragraph was detached. What it said from what it did, what it was from what it held, and over it all something floated....
>
> And so this makes it that Henry James just went on doing what American literature has always done, the form was always the form of the contemporary English one, but the disembodied way of disconnecting something from any thing and anything from something was the

American one. The way it had of often all never having any daily living was an American one.

Some say that it is repression but no it is not repression it is a lack of connection, of there being no connection with living and daily living because there is none, that makes American writing what it always has been and what it will continue to become.[12]

This observation about Henry James has been made since: that his novels, though they take place in a social world, are not about society and that they are not dependent on what happens next in spite of the melodrama, but on what the characters think about what happens, about the inner life, though that life may be grotesquely separated from the events. Indeed, part of the meaning derives from that separation, and that separation is the energy or momentum or moving which is necessary to American writing. As earlier chapters have described, Wilder's words do not create a plot which possesses any intrinsic interest in itself. There is a separation between meaning and event, although ultimately that separation itself becomes the meaning. This does not mean, of course, that Wilder's plotting is not carefully calculated; it does suggest that it has two parts, what is said and what is done.

Gertrude Stein became aware that the language of plays possessed a peculiar nervousness or excitement, distinct from the language of other kinds of writing. The source of the nervousness was separation in many guises. The audience were separated from the action by the curtain and proscenium; they witnessed the event, but they did not participate in it directly. The actors and the characters, as the audience were more or less aware, were never completely fused; always the actor was *playing* the character and consequently was separate from him. There was a gap, sometimes a syncopation between two present times, that of the audience and that of the play. And the scene on the stage, significantly for Gertrude Stein like the scene in a painting, was forcefully in the present tense, as a novel or a poem could never be. It moved. It moved beyond any control of the audience. A reader could read, continue to read, or stop reading a novel in any order he chose, but the audience in a theater could only watch what was happening. The control of life was also missing from the theater because the audience were separated from the event. And although the audience may know the play very well, if they sit in a theater or even choose to read the play, memory, and its kind of control, whether it be the will of conscious memory or the private selection of involuntary memory, is irrelevant. All the audience can do is look at pure event eternally separated from them. As we have seen, Wilder learned to take advantage of all these absolute qualities of the stage, in his characterization, in his narration, and in his plotting. The conclusion of a play is not a *completion* as in life where the person participates in a living climax. In the theater it is a *relief,* seen or heard; the audience relax from the excitement on stage, and there need never be any completion as event so long as the audience are afforded their relief.[13]

Everything that Gertrude Stein observed about the stage and its moving she ultimately used in her efforts to help create an American language, especially one suited to the twentieth century. She was disturbed by the peculiar pleasure derived from witnessing plays in a foreign language that was largely unavailable to her — a pleasure similar to that derived from performances of Shakespeare, where a previous knowledge and a previous appreciation of the poetry and the language counted for little, that is, when they were not absolutely distracting. She was led quite naturally to melodrama, where the language was disconnected from the "silence stillness and quick movement." Just as naturally it was this disconnection of language from event that interested her. "All of a sudden," she wrote, "I began to write Plays."

As anyone who has ever read her plays can say, they are very special in their dialogue and in their plotting.

> Something is always happening, anybody knows a quantity of stories of people's lives that are always happening, there are always plenty for the newspapers and there are always plenty in private life. Everybody knows so many stories and what is the use of telling another story. What is the use of telling a story since there are so many and everybody knows so many and tells so many. . . .
>
> So naturally what I wanted to do in my play was what everybody did not always know nor always tell. . . .
>
> I wanted still more to tell what could be told if one did not tell anything. . . .

I came to think that since each one is that one and that there are a number of them each one being that one, the only way to express this thing each one being that one and there being a number of them knowing each other was in a play. . . . And the idea . . . was to express this without telling what happened, in short to make a play the essence of what happened.[14]

She wished to portray the movement in the verb *to be* without telling a story, the humming of the motor without the movement of the car. Her plays were to be like paintings, like landscapes.

> The landscape has its formation and as after all a play has to have a formation and be in relation one thing to the other thing and as the story is not the thing as any one is always telling something then the landscape not moving but being always in relation, the trees to the hills the hills to the fields the trees to each other any piece of it to any sky and then any detail to any other detail, the story is only of importance if you like to tell or like to hear a story but the relation is there any way.[15]

A new definition of beauty emerged for Wilder from Gertrude Stein's theorizing about plays. George Moore's beautiful language was discarded in favor of a language which as accurately as possible conveyed the intensity of existence, that internal motor. Beauty was created in proportion to how well the language did what it set out to do.

Language, according to Gertrude Stein, did not function as a retailer of stories, though stories might be told. Wilder in his plays has rejected story line almost completely, as in *Our Town* and *The Skin of Our Teeth,* or has treated it as a familiar and friendly cliché in *The Merchant of Yonkers,* or has used as its basis a recognizable myth in *The Alcestiad.* Wilder's many critics who have found his anecdotes naïve, foolish, or stale are measuring his work by a standard he deliberately had given up.

For Wilder as for Gertrude Stein, Americans are not revealed in their most intense being through event. There is only one way for the American to come into relation with other Americans, Wilder wrote, and that is

> when he is united with them in a project, caught up in an idea and propelled with them toward the future. There is no limit to the degree

with which an American is imbued with the doctrine of progress. Place and environment are but *décor* to his journey. He lives not on the treasure that lies about him but on the promises of the imagination.

"I am I," he says, "because my plans characterize me."

Abstract! Abstract![16]

Wilder's characters in this definition are all Americans: George, Emily, Antrobus, Sabina, Mrs. Levi, and Alcestis. They are all planners, schemers, arrangers for the future. What their particular plans are matters very little and may be dependent on events; the intensity of their planning, their total involvement with their planning, is all.

Yielded along with George Moore's beautiful words was the didactic moralizing function of language. Beauty ceased to be persuasion for Wilder. In fact, persuasion had no importance whatever any longer. In the introduction to Gertrude Stein's *Four in America,* Wilder wrote that "the corresponding method of 'description' had broken down" and that "writing must accomplish a revolution whereby it could report things as they were in themselves before our minds had appropriated them and robbed them of their objectivity 'in pure existing.' "[17] Language was asked to establish a continuous present, exclusive of any comment on it. Plays without stories could sometimes do this; Gertrude Stein wrote that from the time of *The Making of Americans* she was engaged in a struggle "to make a whole present of something that it has taken a great deal of time to find out." Once she had found it out, she wrote, "It was a whole there then within me and as such it had to be said."[18] Since plays were made up of a series of moments without progression, but with change in emphasis, her work naturally developed into plays.

The breakdown in description by correspondences is further complicated, as Gertrude Stein saw it, by the failure of total communication accompanied by an ever more desperate effort to persuade. Wilder quotes in his introduction from a conversation with Gertrude Stein:

Why is it that no preachers, no teachers, no orators, no parliamentary debaters ever have any ideas after the age of thirty-five? . . . They get mixed up in their head and think that it is possible for one person to agree totally with another person; and when you think *that* you are lost and never have any ideas any more. Now what we know is formed in our head by thousands of small occasions in the daily life.[19]

He goes on to say that every person's daily occasions are different from those of everybody else. As a result, what becomes important is not "persuasion," but the best presentation of what you know. The greatest compliment from your audience then is for them to say, "Yes, you know it." In the *Paris Review* interview Wilder said:

> The future author is one who discovers that language, the exploitation and manipulation of the resources of the language, will serve him in winning through to his way. This does not necessarily mean that he is highly articulate in persuading or cajoling . . . for this type of [person] . . . is not usually of the "community" type. . . . Language for him is the instrument for digesting experience, for explaining himself to himself.[20]

Wilder here has flatly repudiated his persuasion of beauty through language. In fact, he has denied any sense of audience at all. Like Gertrude Stein, he writes for himself and strangers. His intent is to tell what he knows.

The falsity of persuasion is another legacy of the nineteenth-century English writers, as Gertrude Stein saw it. She wrote that

> it must be understood that explaining was invented, naturally invented by those living a daily island life and owning everything else outside. They owned everything inside of course but that they had always done, but now they owned everything outside and that reinforced their owning everything inside . . . but as they owned everything outside, outside and inside had to be told something about all this owning, otherwise they might not remember all their owning and so there was invented explaining and that made nineteenth century English literature what it is. And with explaining went emotional sentimental feeling. . . .
>
> All this leads you to that what you think is not what you say but you say what you think and you are thinking about what you think.[21]

England's commercial and political success and her desire to secure what had been gained, like so much other success in the modern world, produced sentimental feeling, deception, hypocrisy, and imitation. All of these have been avoided in American writing because of

America's single great virtue: her youth. Applying to all Americans one of youth's most irritating characteristics, the refusal to shoulder responsibility in the tried and true way, Wilder wrote,

> If you have to do a thing, you have lost your freedom. If you have to say a thing, you have lost your sincerity. If you have to love your parent, wife, child, cousin, you begin to be estranged from them already. . . .
>
> Life, life, life is full of things one has to do; and if you have a passion for spontaneity, how do you convert What You Have To Do into the Thing You Choose To Do?
>
> That is one of the most exciting things about being an American and about watching American life: how an American will succeed in converting Necessity into Volition.[22]

As earlier chapters have shown, Americans reject authority, no matter how easy and comfortable the life it provides, for, as Wilder wrote, "Americans do not ask that life present a soothing face. Even if they are in a contented situation they do not hope that life will continue to furnish them More of the Same. They are neither fretful nor giddy, but they are always ready for Something Different."[23] And this chapter will demonstrate later that Americans equally reject the authority conferred by language.

At the same time he was learning from Gertrude Stein, Wilder translated André Obey's *Le Viol de Lucrèce* for Katharine Cornell and adapted Ibsen's *A Doll's House* for Ruth Gordon. In the Ibsen adaptation, he did little more than eliminate from the standard translations the Victorian mannerisms that he thought would be offensive to a modern audience, either because they dated the play or because they seemed to make Ibsen's ideas too awkwardly obvious.

Obey's play is perhaps more important in Wilder's development. Obey's kind of theater also utilizes allegorical characterization, and in the early plays especially, the simplicity and familiarity of the style avoids the usual faults of allegory, the manipulation of cold and mechanical ideas. Wilder's translation was a startling failure. The audience of the time were unable to respond to the "high Roman thirst for decorum,"[24] and the critics could not understand the absence of "a certain Paris chic and rhodomontade."[25] Although the absence of Racine's spirit and the insistence on everyday reality were a disappointment in New York, one of Wilder's friends, who now teaches at the Yale Drama School, recalled thirty years later that a reading Wilder did in his living room after he had completed his translation was one of the finest plays she had ever *seen*. Such praise is surely a rare tribute not only to Wilder's writing skill but to his acting ability as well. And the obvious pleasure Wilder derives from being on the stage, for he has acted in his own plays, or being on the speaker's platform has more than mere personal rewards; his practical experience has helped him to write lines that actors can say. That *Lucrece* appeared "feeble, uncertain and unglamorous"[26] was the fault of the production and the times, not the language.

Just before he translated Obey's play, the volume of one-act plays, *The Long Christmas Dinner, was published*. Among the six plays is the one Wilder calls his favorite, perhaps because it is his first certain and absolute success for the theater using the stage as he wished and saying precisely what he meant. *The Happy Journey to Trenton and Camden* describes a father and a mother, with their two younger children, traveling by automobile from Newark to Camden to visit their married daughter. There is no scenery, and the only properties are a low platform and four chairs which make up the automobile. In the manuscript in the Yale Library the play is subtitled "or *The Portrait of a Lady*." This is a glancing reference to the novel by Henry James and probably also to the poems by Pound and Eliot; but because Wilder's play is so different, it is almost as though he were saying that theirs were not the only kinds of lady. His, unlike those other wealthy and vaguely intellectual ladies, is a firmly middle-class mother, and Wilder has called himself a middle-class playwright, agreeing with Gertrude Stein, when she wrote in *The Making of Americans:*

> Middle-class, middle-class . . . yes here in the heart of a people who despise it, . . . a material middle class who know they are it, with their straight forward bond of family to control it, it is the one thing always human, vital and worthy it — worthy that all monotonously shall repeat it, — and from which has always sprung, and all who really look can see it, the very best the world can ever know, and everywhere we always need it.[27]

The action of the play is described in a line from one of Wilder's Three Minute Plays, *The Warship:* "The best thing for us to do . . . is not to beat our heads . . . but to do our duty where we be."[28] Wilder characterized it as

> a testimonial of homage to the average American mother who brings up her children as instinctively as a bird builds its nest and whose strength lies in the fact that whatever stress arrives from the circumstances of life, she strives to maintain an atmosphere of forward looking industry and readiness.[29]

The problem Wilder set for himself was to find a language recognizable as ordinary middle-class speech but still able to convey feeling and meaning. The dialogue is the speech of anyone, and that is the point. Clichés are clichés precisely because they are so very true on an elementary level. The absence of scenery and properties and the exploitation of the stage as stage both permit the clichéd dialogue and prevent it from being merely banal. The commonplace in such speech is returned to its pristine truth, as though it were being uttered for the first time, and the simple truth of family living is given new life.

The range of such a play is not so narrow as one might expect. Edna St. Vincent Millay rather obtusely complimented Wilder at the play's first performance at the University of Chicago "at having so well pictured that 'detestable bossy kind of mother.' "[30]

The famous lady poet made the mistake of seeing the mother as a real one of a particular type, rather than just mother, bossy or not. The play makes no effort to pretend that what happens on stage is a kind of photograph of the life that outside the theater surrounds the audience. On the contrary, like another play from the same volume, *Queens of France,* it questions that idea.

In *Queens of France,* a New Orleans lawyer, M'su Cahusac, has tricked a number of ladies into believing that each is heir to the French throne. The ladies give him money to continue investigations in support of their claims and to buy royal heirlooms, which are in reality worthless junk. It is possible to imagine that the lawyer is an unpleasant little cheat and that the ladies are poor fools, as, indeed, if we knew them, they would be. But in the play nothing could be farther from

Wilder's intent. Cahusac brings pleasure into the lives of the "Queens" by encouraging dreams in those whose days would otherwise be empty and miserable. Mme. Pugeot speaks for them all: "Oh I am very well, thank you. Excellent. I used to do quite poorly, as you remember, but since this wonderful news I have been more than well, God be praised."[31] Just as the lawyer offers his junk heirlooms, so the playwright presents his lies told in unglamorous and aggressively ordinary speech, and all for our pleasure. Like the "Queens," what the audience need is a little faith; the easiest way not to jeopardize this faith is not to pretend that the fiction is real in the first place, and the junk will do the trick.

In the essay "Toward an American Language," Wilder wrote:

> Elevation and intensity are not solely and inseparably associated with noble images. The sublime does not wear a cothurnus. There are not two doors for words in America, no tradesmen's entrance: all can go in the front door. . . . The United States is a middle class nation and has widened and broadened and deepened the concepts of the wide and the broad and the deep without diminishing the concept of the high.[32]

This does not mean that there is no high feeling, although it certainly changes the expression and even the meaning of that feeling.

The difficulty of conveying elevation and intensity without a set pattern of noble images has confronted the modern writer especially. From the end of the Renaissance it has become increasingly difficult for the writer to provide things with a meaning that does not depend on individual perception of them. Since the middle of the nineteenth century the writer has become almost hysterical in his efforts to present the reality of things exclusive of any conceptualized meaning provided by himself, or as Wilder said of Gertrude Stein's writing, "things as they were in themselves before our minds had appropriated them and robbed them of their objectivity." The scene is littered with victims: Shelley's hallucinations, the art-for-art's sake poets, Gertrude Stein's insistence on a rose being merely a rose, and most recently the new French novels of things are only a few examples. Characteristically, Wilder understands his own problem in terms of the American experience:

Most European exercises in the sublime, in avoiding the common and humble, avoid the specific ... the noble is associated with high vagueness. Audiences which are composed of the selected and the cultivated and the *Gebildete* and *honnêtes gens* and the cognoscenti are not interested in life's diversity; the pressures upon them work toward the formulation of taste and convention and the Rules of the Beautiful and an ever-narrowing purity (i.e., economy) in the selection of detail. But the American public was one and one and one ... to an unlimited number. Their taste could never be codified, for it was overwhelmed by an ever-enlarging vision of the universe and its multifarious character. The bigger the world is, the *less* you can be content with vagueness.[33]

Wilder's difficulty with language is another way of expressing the conflict between Human Nature and the Human Mind. Every writer must discover for himself the words to create a real and recognizable world that is not at the same time so limited as to be trivial and without significance. Wilder first found his detail in a world that has disappeared, but still remains in the memory: barns, kindling wood, drinking troughs, highboys, and hair ribbons. It is this detail, petty and homely but very real, which provides for American audiences the pathos existing in everyone's failure in living. Emily's hair ribbons are not conceptualized; they are hair ribbons. At the same time, they trigger a powerful rush of feeling in the audience.

Wilder wrote that for Americans "concrete things concretely exist, so solidly that these things do not exhale a deep emotion nor invite it. ... Americans do not readily animate things; their tireless imagination is active elsewhere, in the future."[34] The audience were not to sentimentalize over the hair ribbons or the wood-burning stoves; they exist to create a real life for the characters in the play and might just as well have been something else. Gertrude Stein wrote that "nothing changes from generation to generation except the composition in which we live and the composition in which we live makes the art which we see and hear."[35] Emily's hair ribbons are part of Wilder's attempt to prevent the composition in which she lives from being vague and amorphous.

Wilder tossed away all the early ideas of beauty and the sublime, with their purity of diction and meaning, and elaborate metaphors.

The action itself became the metaphor, and Wilder's interest centered on communication through the "thousands of small occasions in the daily life." The cost of making the language suitable to those actions was great. From necessity, the language failed to individualize character in the traditional way. If the characters of *Our Town* are everybody, then their speech, although it is full of specific detail, is also without individual character. Mrs. Gibbs's speech is barely different from Mrs. Webb's or from Emily's.

The absence of the kind of linguistic individuality that has been associated with realistic or classical drama does not mean that the language is not carefully calculated. Many actors have been deceived by the simplicity of the language of *Our Town* into thinking that they might write as well. The actors have embroidered and expanded their parts, writing their own dialogue as they went along in the hope that they would shine more brightly in a larger part. Without exception, they have failed. Such language cannot be invented on the spot at will, and any dialogue added is made at the peril of the actor who attempts it.

Wilder deliberately cultivated speech patterns for his characters that were similar to each other, taking his cue again from Gertrude Stein, for whom people were "separate and yet always repeated."[36] Wilder described the American's ability to count and his pleasure in counting. "To this day, in American thinking, a crowd of ten thousand is not a homogeneous mass of that number, but is one and one and one . . . up to ten thousand."[37] Mrs. Webb and Mrs. Gibbs are separate from each other, and the audience can *see* it, but they resemble each other, too.

Gertrude Stein provided Wilder with an intellectual basis for repeating speech, yet continuing the forward movement of the play. "Every time," she wrote,

> one of the hundreds of times a newspaperman makes fun of my writing and of my repetition he always has the same theme, always having the same theme, that is, if you like, repetition, that is if you like the repeating that is the same thing, but once started expressing this thing, expressing any thing there can be no repetition because the essence of that expression is insistence and if you insist you must each time use empha-

sis and if you use emphasis it is not possible while anybody is alive that they should use exactly the same emphasis....

I became conscious of these things, I suppose anybody does when they first really know that the stars are worlds and that every thing is moving, that is the first conscious feeling of necessary repetition.... Then the second thing is when you first realize the history of various civilizations, that have been on this earth, that too makes one realize repetition and at the same time the difference of insistence.[38]

From this passage it is clear where Wilder learned to understand his archaeological experience in Rome. Also the differences between Jane Crofut's address, ending with "the solar system; the universe; the mind of God," and Stephen Daedalus' on which it is based become apparent. In Joyce there is the feeling of a comforting, if sometimes constricting and ever enclosing, fixed system; in Wilder there is boundlessness and multiplicity.

Most important, through the joke at the expense of the newspapers Gertrude Stein explains the difference between dead repetition and repeating with a varying insistence that is alive. Wilder's dialogue is not created from peculiarities of character, because ultimately his drama is not psychological in the sense of personality. *Our Town* has for one of its central meanings the necessary repetition of experience; this meaning is to be discovered in the quality of the dialogue as well as in what the dialogue says. One character does not merely repeat another. Each, like the succeeding frames on a movie film, is a little bit different, and when they are run in a sequence, they move; they are alive.

James Joyce's writing brought Wilder another example and encouraged his efforts in making a language for *The Skin of Our Teeth*. In the Gerty Macdowell chapter of *Ulysses*, Joyce used a cliché-ridden vocabulary to approximate the empty civilization from which it came. Wilder uses this same idiotic language of cheap magazines and radio serials without Joyce's satiric intent, for he feels that such language can convey meanings that will be understood in spite of its pompous rhetoric, its almost empty vocabulary, and its weak cadences. In a speech he said:

It is true that exaggerations emanating from the realms of advertising are felt when one is in America with a sense almost of the play of complicity of humor and satire, and we know that superlatives fall upon us like rain; and yet it is very American not merely to speak them, but to receive them; and somehow they are divided by ten and passed around like a currency, slightly deflated but understood.[39]

The faults in the language are corrected by some strange mental process. They remain humorous, but the meanings underneath become known. In terms of itself alone, the language cannot be regarded as capable of conveying much meaning; it is when the words are spoken by characters in a play that they assume meaning.

Sabina's idiotic speech can be frightening, as when she announces that Henry-Cain has hit the boy next door with a stone or when she seduces Antrobus.

> Listen, George: *other* people haven't got feelings. Not in the same way that we have. — we who are presidents like you and prizewinners like me. Listen, other people haven't got feelings; they just imagine they have. Within two weeks they go back to playing bridge and going to the movies.
>
> Listen, dear: everybody in the world except a few people like you and me are just people of straw. Most people have no insides at all. Now that you're president you'll see that. Listen, darling, there's a kind of secret society at the top of the world, — like you and me, — that know this. The world was made for us. What's life anyway? Except for two things, pleasure and power, what is life? Boredom! Foolishness. You know it is. Except for those two things, life's nau-se-at-ing. So, — come here. . . .
>
> Now when your wife comes, it's really very simple; just tell her you've decided to get a divorce and marry me.[40]

The horror of this speech exists beyond the situation of the weakness of the flesh. The audience should recognize not simply how easy it is for them to include everybody else in the group who "haven't got feelings" but also how easy it is for them to be included in that group by someone else. Sabina, punctuating her speech with the urgent but uncertain "listen," and in spite of the comic grouping of "presidents" and "prizewinners," sounds like the supporters of the ideas of a master race or white supremacy or of the dangerous and antihuman arguments for any sort of exclusive position for a small group. The empty rhetoric is more pointed by being the language of the least of us, because it eliminates the ease of blaming its horror on the foreign lunacy of a Hitler; theoretically, Sabina's position is well within the possibilities of us all. The speech is emphasized as it follows Sabina's interruption, in the character of Miss Somerset, the actress; she refuses to act out the seduction this evening because a friend of hers who is in the audience has gone through this same experience of losing a husband. She protests at great length and in detail with obvious delight and pleasure, until an actress planted in the audience rushes away in tears. As no words could explain it, this obvious but still comic business has demonstrated the vicious efficacy of her sentimental sympathy. Such shallow and foolish romanticizing possesses dreadful vitality just because it is devoid of thought.

Wilder's meaning is different from Joyce's, and that difference in meaning is part of the difference between the European experience and the American. It is perhaps not unfairly simple to say that Joyce's characters are trapped in a past from which they struggle to escape. This escape, just as in another context Hannah Arendt reads the revolutions of Europe as merely substituting one kind of tyranny for another (unlike the American Revolution), is another trap in disguise. Wilder, agreeing with Joyce's version of Europe's past as a nightmare from which the European cannot awaken, wrote that the European lived

> shut in, above all, with the memories of old oppressions and with the memories of the long bloody revolts against old oppressions, against Authorities and Powers — once awe-inspiring, but now hollow as the bugaboos of infancy — still vestigially present, however, as disavowed menaces and seductions, invitations to escape from the burdens of freedom (Führer! Duce! Commissar!).[41]

And while Sabina illustrates a danger, it is an American one. She does not desire to submit her responsibility and along with it her freedom to some other authority; she misunderstands her responsibility and her freedom. Winning a beauty contest in Atlantic City confers upon her, she thinks, a responsibility so great that other people seem made of straw, so small in comparison are they. She wants only to live up to the promise of her prize; she mistakenly thinks George is part of the promise. She says that "it's really very simple"; George has only to *tell*, to say the words, to Mrs. Antrobus. Sabina and George are the *abstract* Americans Wilder described earlier; planning and talking are equal to achieving more than half the deed.

The Alcestiad is not comic, and although it is based on tragedy, it is not itself a tragedy; moreover, tragedy, according to Wilder, is not suitable to the American's idea of himself, for he is insubmissive to fate and the concept of nobility is foreign. The play requires an attitude of high seriousness, but it should not be remote from the least member of the audience.

The language finally fashioned is a curious one. It is correct, that is, not ungrammatical. It is not the language, however, of the movies and TV, for it is beautifully constructed — vigorous and meaningful. In its extraordinary simplicity, like Alcestis herself, it is almost without personality. Its most distinguishing mark is that it has no distinguishing marks.

In the second act Alcestis has a long speech of farewell when she dies. The vocabulary and the period structure are simple. The speech is entirely lacking in that kind of formal elevation usually associated with the powerful feelings of heroes, though it is full of concrete detail of her life. This speech, after all, is Alcestis' breaking of her silence; one might expect a poetic effect stretched almost to the point of incoherence. Instead Wilder has provided the unadorned: "I have loved you more than life itself."[42] Every member of the audience can understand it, however, especially since it follows a description of the life Alcestis led with Admetus, and that same audience might be mystified at Oedipus' scream of recognition or Hamlet's complicated poetic intuitions. But Alcestis could not speak with the words and authority of the past, for they had lost their power and moreover had become false in the new world.

Americans distrust conventions of any sort, including the conventions of language. How many have worried over the salutation in a letter, feeling that the *dear* was not an accurate counter to the feeling and that whatever form of the name followed it somehow subverted any attempt at creating a tone adequate for the rest of the letter. For Americans the salutation in a letter is false precisely because it is a convention. Life, which is equated with freedom, is wrung out of it. Wilder wrote that it is "difficult to be an American because there is as yet no code, grammar, decalogue by which to orient oneself. Americans are still engaged in inventing what it is to be an American. That is at once an exhilarating and painful occupation."[43]

What is the exhilaration, and what is the pain? Wilder, in the same place, put it another way.

> Fortunately, for several generations the American had the Bible. The Bible . . . is one long contemplation of the situation of the one in the innumerable and it sternly forbids its readers to draw any relief from what lies about them. Its characters hang suspended upon the promises of the imagination. . . . Those to whom destiny has extended a promise and a plan have this consolation, that they feel themselves to be irreplaceable. Each one is a bundle of projects.[44]

To be constantly in process, ever abuilding, with few if any guides, is difficult, overwhelmingly so for some. Americans are constantly searching for a personal truth, which almost always lies in the future. That the search is personal is finally its goal. Americans at their characteristic best are never mistaken for anyone else; each one is constantly making real his own identity separate from any authority that might aid him.

To those who admire the English language written by Englishmen at some fixed period in the past, the American handling of that language is at best ugly and at its worst pernicious and destructive. Americans are breaking the language, which is another aspect of the effort to make the word convey the felt life, the new definition of beauty Wilder learned from Gertrude Stein. Wilder summarized his problem as follows:

> The professional writer treating a narration, though he may put his appreciation of the American into the spoken words of his characters, naturally uses an international language for the portions of sheer exposition; but even there a difference is now setting in. What he asks of

language is, of course, its closeness and proximity to sheer vitality, and what the American soul finds in a word even in the major words of experience — is that the thing has disappeared from behind the word. When a language is new a poet can say "O moon, O ocean!" because the moon and ocean are there, but when a language is old the moon and ocean have disappeared behind the word and it requires particular skill to restore the pure thing to the faded "literary" word.[45]

For Gertrude Stein the problem concerned itself specifically with nouns, although what she described was a more general difficulty. She wrote that

> to name to know how to name earth sea and sky and all that was in them was enough to make them [early poets] live and love in names, and that is what poetry is, it is a state of knowing and feeling a name.[46]
>
> A noun is a name of anything, why after a thing is named write about it. A name is adequate or it is not. If it is adequate then why go on calling it, if it is not then calling it by its name does no good.[47]

Her solution was to call a thing by a name by which it is not known. "Everybody knows that by the way they do when they are in love and a writer should always have that intensity of emotion about whatever is the object about which he writes."[48] This calling a thing by another name passionately in order to feel what is inside that thing is peculiarly American.

> Naturally, and one may say that is what made Walt Whitman naturally that made the change in the form of poetry, that we who had known the names so long did not get a thrill from just knowing them. ... So ... what was there to do. This that I have just described, the creating it without naming it, was what broke the rigid form of the noun.[49]

Gertrude Stein asked for words that could do something, mostly possess the possibility of being mistaken, because "as long as anything does something it keeps alive."[50] Wilder's description of the American use of language is similar.

> Americans are forever putting prepositions and adverbial particles to new uses. ... It is not only an expression of vivacity and energy; it reveals our national tendency to restore to the past its once-present life

rather than to immobilize it, to bury it under the preterite. In narration this assumed a great importance, for Americans wish to declare that all living things are free — and were free.[51]

To celebrate the life in a thing which is its freedom, it is necessary to assert one's independence from the language as it has been written in the past.

Since the American experience according to the American writer is different, his language is different. The apprehension of experience through the ordering of language is for Wilder the beginning as well as the culmination of his art. Everything that I have described in Wilder's plays obviously enough appears in language, and his language is his achievement as well as the act itself.

> Since the American can find no confirmation of identity from the environment in which he lives, since he lives exposed to the awareness of vast distances and innumerable existences, since he derives from a belief in the future the courage that animates him, is he not bent on isolating and "fixing" a value on every existing thing in its relation to a totality, to the All, to the Everywhere, to the Always? And does that not require of him a new way of viewing and feeling and describing any existing thing? And would that not require, in turn, a modification of the language?[52]

Mr. Antrobus inventing the alphabet is not H. C. Earwicker trapped in the experience of Adam. He is, like Emily and George, and Mrs. Levi and Alcestis, constantly creating a new freedom for the future. He is not Joyce's European; he is Wilder's American. Perhaps it is more than fair that Gertrude Stein should, humorously, have the last word here: "There is no use in telling more than you know, no not even if you do not know it."[53]

VI

MYTH

Every novel for sale in a railway station
is the dreaming soul of the human race
telling its story.

ALTHOUGH the emphasis in his plays is on the narration, the sequence of events, Wilder has recognized the need of his audience for a story of some sort. The audience may create the story themselves, but Wilder has provided the clues. Any understanding of Wilder's style will depend, therefore, on the nature of those clues.

The anecdote in Wilder's plays is subservient to its meaning, but Wilder does not spin out ideas or philosophic systems. His abiding interest lies in human nature and its story. To explain what he intended by providing a work for the theater with significance, Wilder told the *Paris Review* interviewer:

> All the greatest dramatists, except the very greatest *one,* have precisely employed the stage to convey a moral or religious point of view concerning the action. . . .
>
> I get around this difficulty by what may be an impertinence on my part. By believing that the moralizing intention resided in the authors as a convention of their times — usually, a social convention so deeply buried in the author's mode of thinking that it seemed to him to be inseparable from creation. . . . I say they injected a didactic intention in order to justify to themselves and to their audiences the exhibition of pure experience.[1]

Wilder is not a pamphleteer; his interest is not in social reform. For him the theater is the place where physical and emotional experience is arranged as effectively and precisely as possible.

In the introduction he wrote for Richard Beer-Hofmann's *Jaakobs Traum*, Wilder explained how myth might resolve the differences between "didactic intention" and the "exhibition of pure experience."

> A myth passing from oral tradition into literature, moves most congenially into poetry and particularly into the poetic drama. Even the most rationalistic reader consents to receive as given the elements of the supernatural and the incredible that are involved in these ancient stories. Their validity rests on the general ideas they contain. . . . The characters whom we have endowed with the life of significant ideas must be endowed with a different kind of life from the realistic — that of the recognizable quotidian.[2]

Characters from myth must be provided with a daily living that is ordinary and common to the audience. The advantage of employing a myth as the basis of a literary work is that it is already equipped with the substance of significant ideas. The anthropologist's and the psychologist's explanations of myth are dismissed as trivial and determined by detail of historical time and geographical place. More important to the artist is the problem of self-knowledge — individual and racial — which is enduring. The persistent elements of myth

> are questions and not answers in regard to the human situation. In the majority of cases the questions seem to have to do with the mind disengaging itself from the passions of finding its true position in the presence of the established authorities, human or divine. They are concretizations of man's besetting preoccupation with the mind and mind's struggle to know itself; and each retelling requires that some answer be furnished to the question that infuses every part of the story.[3]

It is not sufficient to provide the myth with psychology or ordinary rational behavior. No amount of contemporary detail superimposed on the myth can make it significant. Its modernity must be inherent in its story, and the questions it raises must be answered, not finally for all time, but within the artist's comprehension of the world around him. His retelling will be judged by the questions he understands in the myth and the answers he provides to them, his separation of the eternal from the merely ephemeral.

MYTH   117

Myth is well fitted to Wilder's idea of the theater, for it is peculiarly equipped to convey a generalized statement about human beings
who seem themselves to be individualized. The writer need not bother
to provide the characters of myth with details irrelevant to his idea in
order to make the characters real. They are already in possession of a
reality resulting from their existence throughout time. Neither does
the plot concern the writer especially. Of greater importance is the
large idea he sees illustrated in the story that is there. If, as Wilder believes, the anecdote matters only insofar as it illustrates that idea, then
myth is the ideal anecdote because its general outlines are already
known in some way to the audience. A myth is available to everyone.
It is, as Wilder wrote in an essay on Joyce, "the dreaming soul of the
race telling its story." Furthermore, he wrote that the "retelling of
them on every hand occurs because they whisper a validation — they
isolate and confer a significance."[4]

Wilder has really always used a myth as the anecdote for his plays.
The story of Emily's return from the dead is not a classical myth, but
Wilder had used it earlier in *The Woman of Andros* as though it
were. Chrysis recounts it as a myth, and its adaptability to retelling is
further evidence of its mythic quality. *The Merchant of Yonkers* is not
a real myth either, but since its story is based on other works of literature, it is regarded by Wilder as a kind of myth. He, like Pound and
Eliot, uses the writings of others as though they were part of the great
body of ideas available to the entire human group, or in other words
a myth: "Every novel for sale in a railway station is the dreaming soul
of the human race telling its story."[5] *The Skin of Our Teeth* does use
myth; furthermore, it employs history as though it were myth. The
entire play is provided with coherence and additional meaning by its
use of what Wilder would call a recent retelling of a myth, of many
myths, *Finnegans Wake*.

Almost immediately after the opening of *The Skin of Our Teeth*
two articles[6] by Joseph Campbell and Henry Morton Robinson in the
Saturday Review of Literature linked the play with *Finnegans Wake*.
The intent of these two men is not very clear; the tone they assumed,
however, seems from this distance of time inexcusable, and a subse-
quent essay[7] by Robinson made evident his feeling, at least, that Wilder had been dishonest.

Campbell and Robinson wavered between assuming that the play was some sort of literary prank, the fun being able to recognize it, and stating baldly that it was something shoddy masquerading as first-rate. Perhaps this divided attitude indicates a division in the writers. Whatever their intent, when readers of the *Saturday Review of Literature* concluded that Wilder was a plagiarist, neither writer denied that the charge had been their idea in writing the articles. Perhaps the editorial policy of the magazine was at fault. The play, as a result of the two articles, for a while acquired the reputation of being at best unoriginal and derivative and at worst the unsavory work of thievery and plagiarism. Even today, reviews of its performance or comments on it display an uneasiness that can be traced to the *Saturday Review of Literature* articles.

Campbell and Robinson had been working on their *Skeleton Key to Finnegans Wake* and were in an unusually favorable position to recognize Wilder's debt to Joyce. Although they amassed all kinds of evidence to demonstrate the debt, they did not describe, or were unwilling to recognize, its precise nature. *The Skin of Our Teeth* is not, in fact, a dramatization of *Finnegans Wake,* as Edmund Wilson, who was not enthusiastic about the play, immediately recognized.[8]

Wilder never directly answered the two articles, which after all amounted to an attack, though he was painfully aware of them. His few simple and deceptively ingenuous remarks about Joyce and *The Skin of Our Teeth* have not supported his position very much. In 1948 he told an interviewer:

> I embedded one phrase of "Finnegans Wake" into the text as a salute and a bow of homage....
> Sabina mockingly defending her employer, Mr. Antrobus who is also Adam and Everyman, says, "There are certain charges that ought not to be made and, I think I may say, ought not to be allowed to be made." This speech, with its feeble cadence and insecure indignation, is a wonderful example of Joyce's miraculous ear.
> "There are no other lines from Joyce?"
> "None," said Mr. Wilder.[9]

This clears up what was never in doubt really. The disturbing accusation of Campbell and Robinson was not that Wilder lifted lines from *Finnegans Wake,* but that he had adapted Joyce's inspiration and vision. They wrote, "Important plot elements, characters, devices of presentation, as well as major themes and many of the speeches, are directly and frankly imitated."[10] Wilder's statement is no answer to this kind of attack.

It is important first to be reminded that many of the devices and themes that Wilder found in his reading of Joyce he had come across earlier. The notion of circular time, for example, is as easily discovered in Vico's *Scienza Nuova,* where Joyce himself found it. But Gertrude Stein also had been fascinated with the possibilities in this idea, and Dreiser, a still earlier enthusiasm of Wilder's, was too.

In Dreiser's *Laughing Gas* a Doctor Vatabeel undergoes an operation which routinely should be simple, but grows more dangerously complicated as the play progresses. The anesthetic used is laughing gas, hence the title of the play; and it is while under the effect of the gas that the vision of repeated existing is revealed to Vatabeel. He dumbly considers: "In older worlds I have been, worlds like this. I have done this same thing. Society has done all the things it has done over and over."[11]

Vatabeel is pictured as an "endlessly serviceable victim — an avatar,"[12] with progress existing merely as an empty illusion. The urge to life, however, seems to work in him almost in spite of himself, as though it were a reflex action, responding in defiance of his will to the stimulus of the operation. Various Voices urge him to try; he "senses some vast, generic, undecipherable human need."[13] At the same time the rhythm of the universe pounds a "sense of derision of indifference, of universal terror and futility."[14] Demyophon, one of the spirits of the Universe, tells him: "It has no meaning! Over and over! Round and round! . . . What you do now you will do again. And there is no explanation. You are so eager to live — to do it again. Do you not see the humor of that?"[15] And Vatabeel wakes from the gas laughing.

In Dreiser's grotesque play are two ideas that have remained with Wilder throughout his writing career. First and most apparent is the circular and repetitive nature of experience. Second and closely allied with the first is the existence in the individual, race, world, or evolution simultaneously of all experience. Vatabeel not only endlessly repeats experience; he is its avatar as well.

Of course, *Laughing Gas* is just barely literature, and Joyce's novel is one of the great if secret books of our time. Wilder, however, is one of the comparatively few men who have come close to deciphering the mysteries of *Finnegans Wake,* for he has spent hours and hours of his time, especially just before and after the war, reading it, and he possesses the knowledge and the languages to overcome its most obvious difficulties. In 1949 Wilder said at the Goethe Centennial celebration at Aspen, Colorado, that Joyce demonstrates that all the world at all times is one. He continued to say that Joyce did not use the work of others for "allusion, illustration, or ornament," but for "ambience."[16] Here, I think, Wilder has described his own attitude toward the work of Joyce and all his other "sources" as well.

The American writer has the disadvantage of being dependent on Europe (usually) for his culture and history, for the United States has provided relatively little of either commodity. Yet the artist requires both, and Henry James, Pound, Eliot, and Hemingway, to name only a very few, are American writers who made good use of what Europe had to offer without losing their distinctive American spirit.[17] Wilder has made just such use of Joyce, but he has each time heeded Ezra Pound's command to Make It New, for Wilder learned from Ezra Pound how to master the literary as well as the historic past.[18] *Finnegans Wake* provided for Wilder's play a myth of the historical and cultural environment which created America. Its advantages to Wilder may be summed up in his definition of the kind of story a myth is.

First, its "historical authenticity is so far irrelevant as to permit to the narrator an assumption of omniscience in regard to what took place."[19] The writer need not waste any effort establishing the truth of his story. No matter how fantastic the events, they are accepted by the audience as having happened exactly as the writer reports them.

Secondly, a myth is a story "whose antiquity and popular diffusion confer upon it an authority which limits the degree of variation that may be employed in its retelling."[20] The major outlines of the story must be retained to satisfy the audience's pleasure in recognizing the familiar.

Finally, a myth is a story "whose subject matter is felt to have a significance which renders each retelling a contribution to the received ideas of the entire community to which in a very real sense it belongs."[21] Here is the most difficult task for the writer. He must demonstrate his originality, not in the plot, but in the meaning. He must create a significance that does not overstep the limitations of the events that are given, but a significance that is new and contemporary.

It is a serious mistake to assume, as Campbell and Robinson did, that Wilder's play is a rehash of Joyce's novel. Readers of Virgil who come to the *Aeneid* after Homer are inevitably disappointed in Aeneas and utterly fail to understand the Latin epic if they demand another Achilles or Odysseus. Just so puzzled and irritated were Campbell and Robinson when they did not find in Antrobus an exact copy of H. C. Earwicker. In spite of all the parallels between *Finnegans Wake* and *The Skin of Our Teeth* that Campbell and Robinson uncovered, it is careless to conclude, as they did, that Wilder merely collected and catalogued Joyce's discoveries into an adaptation suitable to the Broadway temper. That he had studied and comprehended Joyce's work is certain; but he also succeeded in pervading the whole of his play with his own optimistic and peculiarly American vision of the human animal and his experience through time.

It is not simple patriotism that locates Antrobus and his family in New Jersey. No matter if he is Adam or Noah or Everybody, he is America's version of Man, and unlike Joyce's heroes, he is not determined by his environment, whether it be cultural, physical, or moral. Antrobus is eternally extricating himself from his "ambience" or reinterpreting it or literally changing it. When the American confronts an ice age, he will invent a more efficient way to heat his house.

In 1928 Wilder told André Maurois, "In the whole of the world's literature there are only seven or eight great subjects. By the time of Euripides they had all been dealt with already, and all one can do is to pick them up again.... There is nothing new that a writer can hope to bring except a certain way of looking at life."[22] Wilder brought to the myths of *Finnegans Wake* precisely another way of interpreting them. He saw in Joyce's work another version of the Europe that has been so important to the American writer. Perhaps, as Professor Pearson suggests,[23] the actual experience of Europe has become too commonplace for American writers, but the secondary or literary experience is still available. Through Joyce's novel, Wilder reinterpreted Europe for the

American. Antrobus is free to escape — though with the skin of his teeth only — and create a new independent future. It is more than mere chance, in the light of what the Old World has always dreamed of the United States and perhaps during World War II more realistically expected from it, that *The Skin of Our Teeth* should have presented for a destroyed and to all appearances utterly debilitated Europe a promise for the future. Wilder's play is unquestionably an original work. It portrays the mythic American cheerfully and energetically progressing through a mythic Western civilization.

That the American has no sense of tragedy is perhaps a national flaw, but as Wilder has noted, it is just as surely a major source of national energy. The American has created a new kind of hero, distinct from the tragic hero, and this new hero offers a challenge to American writers for the theater. Using Abraham as an example, Kierkegaard described just such a hero, calling him the religious hero. Wilder's reading of Kierkegaard undoubtedly strengthened his thinking about a theater like ours. "The difference," wrote Kierkegaard,

> between the tragic hero and Abraham is clearly evident. The tragic hero still remains within the ethical. He lets one expression of the ethical find its *telos* in a higher expression of the ethical. . . . Here there can be no question of a teleological suspension of the ethical.[24]

The tragic hero's acts are performed against certain ethical standards that are regarded as being truths. Ordinarily the possession of these ethical standards is possible only in a small closed society, like those of classical Greece or Elizabethan England. In a larger mobile society, like America's, most standards are considered only as existing in relation to others; any absolute is difficult, if not impossible. Wilder wrote:

> Americans constantly feel that the whole world's thinking has to be done over again. They did not only leave the Old World, they repudiated it. Americans start from scratch. . . .
>
> Every American is an autodidact; every American feels himself capable of being the founder of his own religion.[25]

Yet without fixed standards, tragedy is difficult, if not impossible. According to Kierkegaard:

With Abraham the situation was different. By his ... [willingness to sacrifice Isaac] he overstepped the ethical entirely and possessed a higher *telos* outside of it, in relation to which he suspended the former. For I should very much like to know how one would bring Abraham's act into relation with the universal, and whether it is possible to discover any connection whatever between what Abraham did and the universal ... except the fact that he transgressed it. It was not for the sake of saving a people, not to maintain the idea of the state, that Abraham did this, and not in order to reconcile angry deities.[26]

Ethical standards may exist, but for the religious hero they are meaningless because he does not act for others, except as he acts for himself. The usual motives of the tragic hero are absent. Although it is true that Kierkegard was writing Christian philosophy, the application of that philosophy is possible outside Christianity. Wilder has done just this. For him the religious hero is the person who is most intensely alive, the person most intimately related with his everyday existence. The divine is simply that which is unknowable, and it is the unknowable that clarifies everyday living by forcing attention to it. This understanding is not unchristian, but it is more general than most traditional theology would allow.

Kierkegaard wrote also that the "tragic hero accomplishes his act at a definite instant in time."[27] The religious hero's act is performed in "an absolute relation to the absolute," which is not so impersonal as it might first seem, for he is justified by "being the particular individual."[28] The connection between what Wilder learned from Gertrude Stein and what he learned from Kierkegaard is probably most clearly perceptible here. The freedom of Kierkegaard's religious hero is the rootlessness described by Gertrude Stein as the moving in all directions, the absence of a beginning, middle, and end, characteristic of America and the Bible. It is Wilder's "abstract" American and another way of describing the validity of the individual in the face of all the millions who have lived, who are living, and who will live.

The success of Wilder's theater, which has not been recognized because every attempt has been made to measure it against the old standards, is, in fact, that he has helped create new standards. Whether or not we derive pleasure from the theater he has so carefully developed

will probably depend on whether or not we are happy about the political, social, and intellectual changes that have resulted in our time and
country. Wilder, who told the *Paris Review* interviewer, "It would be
a very wonderful thing if we could see more and more works which
close that gulf between highbrows and lowbrows," has attempted to
come to some understanding with what is disparagingly termed "mass
culture." But as Wilder wrote about Emily Dickinson, this does not
necessarily mean directing oneself to the least common denominator,

> for when one has overcome the "low" desire to write for anybody in
> particular — the cultivated, the chosen souls, one's closest friends; when
> one has graduated from all desire to impress the judicious or to appeal
> to the like-minded — then and only then is one released to write for
> Everybody — only then released from the notion that literature is a spe-
> cialized activity, an elegant occupation or a guild secret. For those who
> live in "immensity" it is merely (and supremely) the human voice at its
> purest, and it is accessible to Everybody, not at the literary level, but at
> the human.[29]

It is not, however, easy; and Wilder, perhaps thinking about his own
experience at the hands of critics and audiences as well as Emily Dickinson's, concluded:

> It is Everybody's fault, not hers, if Everybody is not ready to recognize
> it. Perhaps only when Everybody is dead will Everybody be in a condi-
> tion to understand authentic human speech.[30]

It is equally likely that he is thinking of his own Emily's sad return
from death and of the truth she learned there: that the living can never
understand, and in fact can never be expected to understand, completely.

In a speech delivered in Germany in 1957 Wilder said:

> Culture in a democracy has its dangers — but also a duty and a
> promise.
> Through it a new, tremendous theme opens up, which must be de-
> scribed, deeply thought out, expressed and explored: Man with his head
> up.
> This attitude and this expectation can be confusing as the works of
> literature of the last years have shown us. They can even lead to despair.

Democracy has a great duty: to create new myths, new metaphors, and new images and to show the new condition of dignity into which Man is entering.[31]

Wilder's work has exhibited one direction which the new myths, the new metaphors, and the new forms may take to illuminate man's new position. He has examined Europe's past, and he has brought a new answer to the questions it asks. He has explored a new idea of the theater; not by any means the only one, but one that gives evidence of providing a way for the future.

APPENDIX

Mrs. Levi and part of the first act of *The Merchant of Yonkers* have their source in Molière's *L'Avare*. The following is a comparison of the two texts.

VANDERGELDER: . . . Good morning, Mrs. Levi.

MRS. LEVI: Oh, Mr. Vandergelder, how handsome you look! You take my breath away. — . . . Oh, Mr. Vandergelder, I wish Irene Molloy could see you now. But then! I don't know what's come over you lately. You seem to be growing younger every day.

VAN.: Allowing for exaggeration, Mrs. Levi. Eh, eh. If a man eats careful there's no reason why he should look old.

MRS. L.: You never said a truer word.

VAN.: I won't see fifty-five again, Mrs. Levi.

MRS. L.: Ha! Fifty-five! What are you saying! Fifty-five's a *man's* age,

HARPAGON: . . . Hé bien! qu'est-ce, Frosine?

FROSINE: Ah! mon Dieu! que vous vous portez bien! et que vous avez là un vrai visage de santé!

HARP.: Qui, moi?

FROS.: Jamais je ne vous vis un teint si frais et si gaillard.

HARP.: Tout de bon?

FROS.: Comment? vous n'avez de votre vie été si jeune que vous êtes; et je vois des gens de vingt-cinq ans qui sont plus vieux que vous.

HARP.: Cependant, Frosine, j'en ai soixante bien comptés.

FROS.: Hé bien! qu'est-ce que cela, soixante ans? Voilà bien de quoi! C'est la fleur de l'âge cela, et

that's what it is, — sense, strength, judgment —

VAN.: Well, that's true anyway. But I sometimes think I could do with ten years less.

MRS. L.: You're joking. Ha-ha-ha. Why, I can see at a glance that you're the stuff that will be shouting and stamping about at a hundred, — and eating five meals a day, like my uncle Harry. At fifty-five my uncle Harry was a mere boy. I'm a judge of hands, Mr. Vandergelder; show me your hand. Lord in Heaven! What a lifeline!

VAN.: Where?

MRS. L.: Just look at it.

VAN.: Eh, eh!

MRS. L.: From *here* to *here*. It runs right off your hand. I don't know where it goes. Ha-ha-ha. They'll have to hit you on the head with a mallet. Ha-ha-ha.

VAN.: Now, Mrs. Levi!

MRS. L.: They'll have to stifle you with a sofa-pillow. Ha-ha-ha.

vous entrez maintenant dans la belle saison de l'homme.

HARP.: Il est vrai; mais vingt années de moins pourtant ne me feroient point de mal, que je crois.

FROS.: Vous moquez-vous? Vous n'avez pas besoin de cela, et vous êtes d'une pâte a vivre jusques à cent ans.

HARP.: Tu le crois!

FROS.: Assurément. Vous en avez toutes les marques. Tenez-vous un peu. Oh! que voilà bien là, entre vos deux yeux, un signe de longue vie!

HARP.: Tu te connois à cela?

FROS.: Sans doute. Montrez-moi votre main. Ah! mon Dieu! quelle ligne de vie!

HARP.: Comment?

FROS.: Ne voyez-vous pas jusqu'où va cette ligne-là?

HARP.: Hé bien! qu'est-ce que cela veut dire?

FROS.: Par ma foi! je disois cent ans; mais vous passerez les six-vingts.

HARP.: Est-il possible?

FROS.: Il faudra vous assommer,

(VANDERGELDER *laughs unwillingly*.)

MRS. L.: You'll bury us all. — However, to return to our business. Mr. Vandergelder, I've found the most wonderful girl for you. The ideal wife.[1]

VAN.: . . . Hm. How old is she?

MRS. L.: Nineteen, say twenty.

VAN.: Twenty, Mrs. Levi?

MRS. L.: And pretty as a picture. Little ankles; adorable little face . . .

VAN.: Twenty, Mrs. Levi. Girls

vous dis-je; et vous mettrez en terre et vos enfants, et les enfants de vos enfants.

HARP.: Tant mieux. Comment va notre affaire?

FROS.: Faut-il le demander? et me voit-on mêler de rien dont je ne vienne à bout? J'ai surtout pour les mariages un talent merveilleux; il n'est point de partis au monde que je ne trouve en peu de temps le moyen d'accoupler; et je crois, si je me l'étois mis en tête, que je marierois le Grand Turc avec la République de Venise. Il n'y avoit pas sans doute de si grandes difficultés à cette affaire-ci. Comme j'ai commerce chez elles, je les ai à fond l'une et l'autre entretenues de vous, et j'ai dit à la mère le dessein que vous avíez conçu pour Mariane, à la voir passer dans la rue, et prendre l'air à sa fenêtre.[2]

HARP.: Mais, Frosine, il y a encore une chose qui m'inquiète. La fille est jeune, comme tu vois; et les jeunes gens d'ordinaire n'aiment que leurs semblables, ne cherchent que leur compagnie. J'ai peur qu'un homme de mon âge ne soit pas de son goût; et que cela ne vienne à produire chez moi certains petits désordres qui ne m'accommoderoient pas.

FROS.: Ah! que vois la connoissez mal! C'est encore une particularité

of twenty are apt to favor young fellows of their own age.

MRS. L.: But you don't listen to me. And you don't know the girl. Mr. Vandergelder, she has a positive horror of flighty, brainless young men. What she likes is a man of *sense,* her own words. None of these livery-stable loungers, she said; with their green derby hats, she said, and their onyx-head canes, throwing their money away in bowling-alleys. No, sir: I like a man that's settled. In so many words, she said it. A fine head of gray hair is worth twenty shined up with goose-grease. And, Mr. Vandergelder, I want to warn you right now not to set about making yourself any younger, or she'll start looking about for a man that's more to her taste.

VAN.: That's . . . that's not usual, Mrs. Levi.

MRS. L.: Usual? I'm not wearing myself to the bone hunting up *usual* girls to interest you, Mr. Vandergelder. Usual, indeed. Listen to me: do you know the pictures she has on her wall? Is it any of these Romeos and Lochinvars? No! — it's Moses on the mountain, that's what she's

que j'avois à vous dire. Elle a une aversion épouvantable pour tous les jeunes gens, et n'a de l'amour que pour les vieillards.

HARP.: Elle?

FROS.: Oui, elle. Je voudrois que vous l'eussiez entendu parler là-dessus. Elle ne peut souffrir du tout la vue d'un jeune homme; mais elle n'est point plus ravie, dit-elle, que lorsqu'elle peut voir un beau vieillard avec une barbe majestueuse. Les plus vieux sont pour elle les plus charmants, et je vous avertis de n'aller pas vous faire plus jeune que vous êtes. Elle veut tout au moins qu'on soit sexagénaire; et il n'y a pas quatre mois encore, qu'étant prête d'être mariée, elle rompit tout net le mariage, sur ce que son amant fit voir qu'il n'avoit que cinquante-six ans, et qu'il ne prit point de lunettes pour signer le contrat.

HARP.: Sur cela seulement?

FROS.: Oui. Elle dit que ce n'est pas contentement pour elle que cinquante-six ans; et surtout, elle est pour les nez qui portent des lunettes.

HARP.: Certes, tu me dis là une chose toute nouvelle.

FROS.: Cela va plus loin qu'on ne vous peut dire. On lui voit dans sa

got. Benjamin Franklin on his cane. Hanging right above her dear little white bed. If you want to make her happy you give her a picture of Methusala surrounded by his grandchildren, that's my advice to you.

VAN.: Allowing for exaggeration, Mrs. Levi.

MRS. L.: If I exaggerate, may I lose my tongue.[3]

chambre quelques tableaux et quelques estampes; mais que pensez-vous que ce soit: Des Adonis? des Céphales? des Pâris? et des Apollons? Non: de beaux portraits de Saturne, du roi Priam, du vieux Nestor, et du bon père Anchise sur les épaules de son fils.

HARP.: Cela est admirable! Voilà ce que je n'aurois jamais pensé; et je suis bien aisé d'apprendre qu'elle est de cette humeur. En effet, si j'avois été femme, je n'aurois point aimé les jeunes hommes.

FROS.: Je le crois bien. Voilà de belles drogues que des jeunes gens, pour les aimer! Ce sont de beaux morveux, de beaux godelureaux, pour donner envie de leur peau; et je voudrois bien savoir quel ragoût il y a à eux.

HARP.: Pour moi, je n'y en comprends point; et je ne sais pas comment il y a des femmes qui les aiment tant.

FROS.: Il faut être folle fieffée. Trouver la jeunesse aimable! est-ce avoir le sens commun? Sont-ce des hommes que de jeunes blondins? et peut-on s'attacher à ces animaux-là?

HARP.: C'est ce que je dis tous les jours: avec leur ton de poule laitée, et leurs trois petits brins de barbe relevés en barbe de chat, leurs per-

ruques d'étoupes, leurs hauts-de-
chausses tout tombants, et leurs es-
tomacs débraillés.

Fros.: Eh! cela est bien bâti, au-
près d'une personne comme vous.
(*To the audience.*) Voilà un
homme cela. Il y a là de quoi satis-
faire à la vue; et c'est ainsi qu'il faut
être fait, et vêtu, pour donner de
l'amour.

Harp.: Tu me trouves bien?

Fros.: Comment? vous êtes à ra-
vir, et votre figure est à peindre.
Tournez-vous un peu, s'il vous plaît.
Il ne se peut pas mieux. Que je vous
voie marcher. (*To the audience.*)
Voilà un corps taillé, libre, et dé-
gagé comme il faut, et qui ne mar-
que aucune incommodité.

Harp.: Je n'en ai pas de grandes,
Dieu merci. Il n'y a que ma fluxion,
qui me prend de temps en temps.

Fros.: Cela n'est rien. Votre fluxion ne vous sied point mal, et vous
avez grâce à tousser.

Harp.: Dis-moi un peu: Mariane
ne m'a-t-elle point encore vu? N'a-
t-elle point pris garde à moi en passant?

Fros.: Non; mais nous nous som-
mes fort entretenues de vous. Je lui
ai fait un portrait de votre per-

VAN.: I hope ... hm ... that she has some means, Mrs. Levi. I have a large household to run.

MRS. L.: Ernestina! She's worth her weight in gold. She'll bring you five thousand a year.

VAN.: Eh, eh!

MRS. L.: Listen to me, Mr. Vandergelder, you're a man of sense. I hope; a man that can reckon. In the first place, she's an orphan. She's been brought up with a great saving of food. Yes, sir. — At the same time that she cooks perfect miracles for her friends, what does she eat herself? Apples and lettuce. It's what she's been used to eat and it's what she likes best. She saves you two thousand a year right there. Secondly, she makes her own clothes, and she's the best dressed woman on Brooklyn Heights this minute. She thanks God that she's warm-blooded, and she goes to the market dressed in a raincoat that her uncle got in the War. She saves you a thousand dollars right there. Thirdly, her health is of iron —

sonne; et je n'ai pas manqué de lui vanter votre mérite, et l'avantage que ce lui seroit d'avoir un mari comme vous.[4]

HARP.: Mais, Frosine, as-tu entretenu la mère touchant le bien qu'elle peut donner à sa fille? Lui as-tu dit qu'il falloit qu'elle s'aidât un peu, qu'elle fît quelque effort, qu'elle se saignât pour une occasion comme celle-ci? Car encore n'épouse-t-on point une fille, sans qu'elle apporte quelque chose.

FROS.: Comment? c'est une fille qui vous apportera douze mille livres de rente.

HARP.: Douze mille livres de rente!

FROS.: Oui. Premièrement, elle est nourrie et élevée dans une grande épargne de bouche; c'est une fille accoutumée à vivre de salade, de lait, de fromage et des pommes, et à laquelle par conséquent il ne faudra ni table bien servie, ni consommés exquis, ni orges mondés perpétuels, ni les autres délicatesses qu'il faudroit pour une autre femme; et cela ne va pas à si peu de chose, qu'il ne monte bien, tous les ans, à trois mille francs pour le moins. Outre cela, elle n'est curieuse que d'une propreté fort simple, et n'aime point les superbes habits, ni les riches bijoux, ni les

Van.: But, Mrs. Levi, that's not money in the pocket.

Mrs. L.: We're talking about marriage, aren't we, Mr. Vandergelder? The money she saves while she's in Brooklyn is none of your affair, but if she were your wife that would be *money*. Yes, sir, that's money.

Van.: Hm! Hm!...[5]

Mrs. L.: Really, come to think of it, I don't see where I could get the time. I'm so busy over that wretched law-suit of mine. Yes. If

meubles somptueux, où donnent ses pareilles avec tant de chaleur; et cet article-là vaut plus de quatre mille livres par an. De plus, elle a une aversion horrible pour le jeu, ce qui n'est pas commun aux femmes d'aujourd'hui; et j'en sais une de nos quartiers qui a perdu, à trente-et-quarante, vingt mille francs cette année. Mais n'en prenons rien que le quart. Cinq mille francs au jeu par an, et quatre mille francs en habits et bijoux, cela fait neuf mille livres; et mille écus que nous mettons pour la nourriture, ne voilà-t-il pas par année vos douze mille francs bien comptés?

Harp.: Oui, cela n'est pas mal; mais ce compte-là n'est rien de réel.

Fros.: Pardonnez-moi. N'est-ce pas quelque chose de réel, que de vous apporter en mariage une grande sobriété, l'héritage d'un grand amour de simplicité de parure, et l'acquisition d'un grand fonds de haine pour le jeu?

Harp.: C'est une raillerie, que de vouloir me constituer son dot de toutes les dépenses qu'elle ne fera point. Je n'irai pas donner quittance de ce que je ne reçois pas; et il faut bien que je touche quelque chose.[6]

Fros.: J'aurois, Monsieur, une petite prière à vous faire. (*Il prend un air sévère.*) J'ai un procès que je suis sur le point de perdre, faute

I win it, I don't mind telling you, I'll be what's called a very rich woman. I'll own half of Staten Island, that's a fact. But just now I'm at my wits' ends for a little help, just enough money to finish it off. My wits' end. (*In order not to hear this* VANDERGELDER *has a series of coughs, sneezes and minor convulsions.*) But perhaps I could arrange a little dinner; I'll see. Oh, Mr. Vandergelder, I can't wait for you to lay eyes on her. A treasure. A dove. And what a foot! Smaller than mine, if I do say it. Never wears a dress lower than this — (*Strikes her chin.*) — no one has ever seen more than that, her own mother hasn't. — Yes, for that law-suit all I need is fifty dollars, and Staten Island's as good as mine. Now I'm an old friend of yours and your wife's. I've been trotting all over New York for *you,* trying to find you a suitable wife.

VAN.: Fifty dollars!!

d'un peu d'argent; et vous pourriez facilement me procurer le gain de ce procès, si vous aviez quelque bonté pour moi. (*Il reprend un air gai.*) Vous ne sauriez croire le plaisir qu'elle aura de vous voir. Ah! que vous lui plairez! et que votre fraise à l'antique fera sur son esprit un effet admirable! Mais surtout elle sera charmée de votre haut-de-chausses, attaché au pourpoint avec des aiguillettes: c'est pour la rendre folle de vous; et un amant aiguilleté sera pour elle un ragoût merveilleux.

HARP.: Certes, tu me ravis de me dire cela.

FROS.: (*Il reprend son visage sévère.*) En vérité, Monsieur, ce procès m'est d'une conséquence tout à fait grande. Je suis ruinée, si je le perds; et quelque petite assistance me rétabliroit mes affaires. (*Il reprend un air gai.*) Je voudrois que vous eussiez vu le ravissement où elle étoit à m'entendre parler de vous. La joie éclatoit dans ses yeux, au récit de vos qualités; et je l'ai mise enfin dans une impatience extrême de voir ce mariage entièrement conclu.

HARP.: Tu m'as fait grand plaisir, Frosine; et je t'en ai, je te l'avoue, toutes les obligations de monde.

FROS.: (*Il reprend son air sérieux.*) Je vous prie, Monsieur, de me

Mrs. L.: Two whole months I've been —

Van.: Fifty dollars, Mrs. Levi ... is no joke. I don't know where money's gone to these days. It's in hiding. . . . There's twenty. . . . There's, uh twenty-five. I can't spare more than that, not now, I can't.

Mrs. L.: Well, this will help, — help somewhat.[7]

donner le petit secours que je vous demande. Cela me remettra sur pied, et je vous en serai éternellement obligée.

Harp.: Adieu. Je vais achever mes dépêches.

Fros.: Je vous assure, Monsieur, que vous ne sauriez jamais me soulager dans un plus grand besoin.

Harp.: Je mettrai ordre que mon carrosse soit tout prêt pour vous mener à la foire.

Fros.: Je ne vous importunerois pas, si je ne m'y voyois forcée par la nécessité.

Harp.: Et j'aurai soin qu'on soupe de bonne heure, pour ne vous point faire malades.

Fros.: Ne me refusez pas la grâce dont je vous sollicite. Vous ne sauriez croire, Monsieur, le plaisir que ...

Harp.: Je m'en vais. Voilà qu'on m'appelle. Jusqu'à tantôt. (*Exit.*)

Fros.: Que la fièvre te serre, chien de vilain à tous les diables! Le ladre a été ferme à toutes mes attaques; mais il ne me faut pas pourtant quitter la négociation; et j'ai l'autre côtè, en tout cas, d'où je suis assurée de tirer bonne récompense.[8]

NOTES

PREFACE: EVERYBODY'S THORNTON WILDER

1. Malcolm Cowley, ed., *Writers at Work* (New York, 1958), pp. 108 f.

2. Richard Boleslavsky, *Acting, The First Six Lessons* (New York, 1933), p. 82.

I: THE SAVOR OF LIFE

1. Theodore Dreiser, *Plays of the Natural and the Supernatural* (New York, 1916), p. 172.

2. Thornton Wilder, *The Angel That Troubled the Waters* (New York, 1928), p. 102.

3. *Ibid.*

4. Thornton Wilder, *The Woman of Andros* (New York, 1930), p. 35.

5. First manuscript version of *Our Town*, Yale Library Collection of American Literature. Only Acts I and III are available.

6. Thornton Wilder, *Our Town*, in *Three Plays* (New York, 1957), p. 101.

7. Uncatalogued letter to Mrs. G. P. Baker, dated March, 1938, Yale Library Collection of American Literature.

8. *Our Town*, p. 103.

9. First manuscript version of *Our Town*.

10. *Our Town*, p. 91.

11. Thornton Wilder, *Heaven's My Destination* (New York, 1935), p. 219.

12. *Ibid.*, p. 290.

13. Conversation with Mr. Wilder.

14. Manuscript of *The Woman of Andros*, Yale Library Collection of American Literature.

15. Typescript of *Sloth*, in the possession of Mr. Wilder.

16. *Ibid.*

17. Conversation with Mr. Wilder. The ending is often incorrectly printed in the various editions, omitting the "sitting quietly at home," thereby changing the play's emphasis to adventure alone.

18. *Our Town*, p. 100.

19. Thornton Wilder, *The Merchant of Yonkers* (New York, 1939), p. 30.

20. Thornton Wilder, *The Matchmaker*, in *Three Plays* (New York, 1957), pp. 395 f.

21. *The Merchant of Yonkers*, pp. 20 f.

22. *Ibid.*, p. 21.

23. *The Matchmaker*, p. 172.

24. *Ibid.*, p. 173.

25. *The Merchant of Yonkers*.

26. Quoted in "An Obliging Man," *Time*, LXI (January 12, 1953), 48.

27. Quoted in Eric Wollencott Barnes, *The Man Who Lived Twice* (New York, 1956), p. 221.

28. Thornton Wilder, *The Skin of Our Teeth*, in *Three Plays* (New York, 1957), p. 242.

29. *Ibid.*, p. 244.

30. *Ibid.*, p. 245.

31. *Ibid.*, pp. 200 f.

32. *Ibid.*, p. 167.

33. Malcolm Cowley, ed., *Writers at Work* (New York, 1958), pp. 114 f.

34. *Ibid.*

35. *The Skin of Our Teeth*, p. 248.

II: THE RELIGIOUS LIFE

1. Thornton Wilder, *The Angel That Troubled the Waters* (New York, 1928), p. xv.

2. Thornton Wilder, "The Trumpet Shall Sound . . . Act Four," *Yale Literary Magazine*, LXXXV (January, 1920), 198.

3. Manuscript of *The Woman of Andros*, Yale Library Collection of American Literature.

4. Thornton Wilder, *The Bridge of San Luis Rey* (New York, 1927), p. 220.

5. *Ibid.*, p. 84.

6. *Ibid.*, p. 235.

7. *Ibid.*, p. 23.

8. Thornton Wilder, *A Thornton Wilder Trio* (New York, 1956), p. 19.

9. Michael Gold, "Wilder: Prophet of the Genteel Christ," *New Republic*, LXIV (October 22, 1930), 266–267.

10. Mary McCarthy, *Sights & Spectacles* (New York, 1956), p. x.

11. Thornton Wilder, *The Skin of Our Teeth*, in *Three Plays* (New York, 1957), pp. 249 f.

12. Thornton Wilder, *Our Town*, in *Three Plays* (New York, 1957), p. 45.

13. Quoted in Donald Gallup, ed., *The Flowers of Friendship* (New York, 1953), p. 304.

14. Gertrude Stein, *Four in America* (New Haven, 1947), p. xvi.

15. Donald Sutherland, *Gertrude Stein* (New Haven, 1951), p. 123.

16. Malcolm Cowley, ed., *Writers at Work* (New York, 1958), p. 104.

17. Thornton Wilder, *The Woman of Andros* (New York, 1930), p. 79.

18. Sophocles, *Oedipus the King*, tr. Francis Storr (New York, 1955), pp. 12 f.

19. *Ibid.*, p. 10.

20. Wilder told a magazine interviewer in 1948: "All my life I have passed from enthusiasm to enthusiasm and gratitude to gratitude. *The Ides of March*, my new novel, can be said to be written under the sign of Kierkegaard." Quoted in Robert van Gelder, "Interview with a Best-Selling Author: Thornton Wilder," *Cosmopolitan*, CXXIV (April, 1948), 120.

21. *Ibid.*

22. *Ibid.*

23. Typescript of *The Alcestiad*, in the possession of Mr. Wilder, p. 2:23.

24. S. Kierkegaard, *Fear and Trembling*, tr. Walter Lowrie (Princeton, 1941), p. 64.

25. *The Alcestiad*, p. 2:25.

26. Hercules accuses himself of Kierkegaard's idea of despair at not willing to become oneself, the refusal to recognize one's relationship with God. Kierkegaard wrote: "To become oneself is to become concrete. But to

become concrete means neither to become finite nor infinite, for that which is to become concrete is a synthesis. Accordingly the development consists in moving away from oneself infinitely by the process of infinitizing oneself, and in returning to oneself infinitely by the process of finitizing. If on the contrary the self does not become itself, it is in despair, whether it knows it or not. . . . Not to be one's own self is despair." S. Kierkegaard, *The Sickness unto Death,* tr. Walter Lowrie (Princeton, 1941), p. 44.

27. *The Alcestiad,* pp. 1:3–1:5.

28. For example, Egisthe in Giraudoux's *Electre* cynically says in the first act: "Je crois aux dieux. Ou plutôt je crois que je crois aux dieux. Mais je crois en eux non pas comme en de grandes attentions et de grandes surveillances, mais comme en de grandes distractions. Entres les espaces et les durées, toujours en flirt, entre les gravitations et les vides, toujours en lutte, il est de grandes indifférences qui sont les dieux. Je les imagine, non point occupés sans relâche de cette moisissure suprême et mobile de la terre qu'est l'humanité, mais parvenus à un tel grade de sérénité et d'ubiquité qu'il ne peut plus être que la béatitude, c'est-à-dire l'inconscience. Ils sont inconscients au sommet de l'échelle de toutes créatures comme l'atome est inconscient à leur degré le plus bas. La différence est que c'est une inconscience fulgurante, omnisciente, taillée à mille-faces et, à leur état normal des diaments atones et sourds, ils ne repondent qu'aux lumières qu'aux signes et sans les comprendre." Jean Giraudoux, *Electre* (Paris, 1937), pp. 39 f.

29. *The Alcestiad,* p. 1:20.

30. *Ibid.*

31. *Ibid.,* p. 1:3.

32. *Ibid.,* pp. 1:22 f.

33. *Ibid.,* pp. 1:25 f.

34. *Ibid.,* p. 1:12.

35. *The Sickness unto Death,* pp. 209 f.

36. *Ibid.,* p. 199.

37. *Ibid.,* pp. 48 f.

38. *The Alcestiad,* pp. 1:26 f.

39. *Ibid.,* p. 1:27.

40. *Fear and Trembling,* p. 22.

41. *The Alcestiad,* p. 2:6.

42. *The Sickness unto Death,* pp. 207 ff.

43. *Ibid.,* pp. 210 f.

44. *Ibid.,* p. 209.

45. *The Alcestiad,* p. 3:5.

46. *Ibid.,* p. 3:24.

47. *Ibid.,* p. 3:25.

48. *Ibid.,* p. 3:26.

49. *Fear and Trembling,* pp. 55 ff. Italics mine.

50. *The Angel That Troubled the Waters,* p. xv.

51. Thornton Wilder, "A Time of Troubles," *Academy Papers,* Addresses on the Evangeline Wilbour Blashfield Foundation, II (New York, 1951), pp. 219 f.

III: ALL TIMES AND ALL PLACES

1. Cesare Pavese, for example, despairingly speaks of the difference between American and European feeling for place: "And yet the country [the United States] was big, there was enough in it for everybody. There were women, there was land, there was money. But nobody had enough of it, nobody ever stopped no matter how much he had, and the fields and the vineyards, too, were like public parks, artificial flower beds like the ones at railroad stations, or else uncultivated parched land, cast-iron mountains. It wasn't a country where a man could be resigned, rest his head and say to the others, 'For better or worse, you know me. For better or worse, let me live.' That was the frightening part. Even among themselves, they didn't know each other. When you crossed those mountains you realized at every turn that no one had ever stopped there, nobody had put a hand to them." Cesare Pavese, *The Moon and the Bonfires,* tr. Marrianne Ceconi (New York, 1953), p. 20.

2. Norman Holmes Pearson, "The American Writer and the Feeling for Community," *Some American Studies* (Kyoto, 1964), p. 21.

3. Thornton Wilder, "Toward an American Language," *Atlantic,* CXC (July, 1952), 32.

4. Thornton Wilder, "Joyce and the Modern Novel," *A James Joyce Miscellany* (n.p., 1957), pp. 13 f.

5. Thornton Wilder, *A Thornton Wilder Trio* (New York, 1956), p. 9.

6. Thornton Wilder, "Some Thoughts on Playwriting," in Augusto Centeno, ed., *The Intent of the Artist* (Princeton, 1941), p. 96.

7. Quoted in Donald Gallup, ed., *The Flowers of Friendship* (New York, 1953), p. 305.

8. Quoted in "An Obliging Man," *Time,* LXI (January 12, 1953), 46.

9. Malcolm Cowley, ed., *Writers at Work* (New York, 1958), p. 113.

10. *Ibid.*, p. 114.

11. Thornton Wilder, *Our Town*, in *Three Plays* (New York, 1957), p. 6.

12. *Ibid.*, p. 8.

13. *Ibid.*, p. 10.

14. Thornton Wilder, "The American Loneliness," *Atlantic*, CXC (August, 1952), 68.

15. *Our Town*, p. 32.

16. *Ibid.*

17. Thornton Wilder, *The Skin of Our Teeth*, in *Three Plays* (New York, 1957), p. 151.

18. *Ibid.*, p. 152.

19. *Ibid.*, p. 228.

20. *Ibid.*, p. 227.

21. In 1954 Wilder wrote: "Freud once said to me, 'Oh, I don't think that writers will be able to use the tenets of psychoanalysis for two or three hundred years. Numbers of my friends — Arnold Zweig and Stefan Zweig and Frank Werfel — have been using psychoanalysis in their novels; but it still comes out as clinical document, as schemata. Only in two or three hundred years will the *Dichter* have assimilated it at so deep a level that they'll know it without knowing they know it. And it will come out as pure novel.' " "Joyce and the Modern Novel," p. 16.

22. *Ibid.*, pp. 18 f.

23. " 'Our Town' — From Stage to Screen," *Theatre Arts*, XXIV (November, 1940), 815.

24. Gerald Weales, "Unfashionable Optimist," *Commonweal*, LXVII (February 7, 1958), 487.

25. Thornton Wilder, "A Preface for 'Our Town,' " New York *Times*, February 13, 1938, sec. 2, p. 1.

26. *Our Town*, p. 32.

27. Gertrude Stein, *The Making of Americans* (New York, 1934), p. 211.

28. Lewis Morton, "An Experiment in Classicism," *American Review*, IV (March, 1935), 578.

29. Alfred Jarry, *Œuvres complètes*, v. 4 (Lausanne, n.d.), p. 159.

30. *Ibid.*, v. 7, letter dated October 30, 1894, p. 270.

31. *Our Town*, p. 5.

32. *Ibid.*

33. Robert van Gelder, "Interview with a Best-Selling Author: Thornton Wilder," *Cosmopolitan*, CXXIV (April, 1948), 123.

34. Jarry would present "à ces cinq cents bons esprits ce qu'on prodigue aux auditeurs de M. Donnay [a popular author of thesis plays], le repos de ne pas voir sur la scène ce qu'ils ne comprennent pas, le plaisir actif de créer aussi un peu à mesure et de prévoir.

"Ce qui est un index de quelques objets notoirement horrible et incompréhensible pour ces cinq cents esprits et qui encombrent la scène sans utilité, en premier rang le décor....

"Le décor est hybride, ni naturel ni artificiel. S'il était semblable à la nature, ce serait un duplicata superflu. . . . On parlera plus loin de la nature décor. Il n'est pas artificiel en ce sens qu'il ne donne à l'artiste la réalisation de l'extérieur vu à travers soi ou mieux créé par soi....

"Et il est juste que chaque spectateur voie la scène dans le décor qui convient à sa vision de la scène. Devant un grand public, différemment, n'importe quel décor artiste est bon, la foule comprenant ne de soi, mais d'autorité....

"Nous ne reviendrons pas sur la question entendue un fois pour toutes de la stupidité du trompe-l'œil. Mentionnons que ledit trompe-l'œil fait allusion à celui qui voit grossièrement, c'est à dire ne voit pas, et scandalise qui voit d'une façon intelligente et éligente [?] la nature, lui en présentant la caricature par celui qui ne comprend pas. Zeuxis a trompé des bêtes brutes, dit on, et Titien un aubergiste.

"Le décor par celui qui ne sait pas peindre approche plus du décor abstrait, n'en donnant que la substance; comme aussi le décor qu'on saurait simplifier en choisirait les utiles accidents.

"Nous avons essayé des décors *héraldiques,* c'est à dire désignant d'une teinte unie et uniforme toute une scène ou un acte, les personnages passant harmoniques sur ce champ de blason. Cela est un peu puérile, ladite teinte d'établissant seule (et plus exacte, car il faut tenir compte du daltonisme universel et de toute idiosyncrasie) sur un fond qui n'a pas de couleur. On se le procure simplement d'une manière symboliquement exacte avec une toile pas peinte ou un envers de décor, chacun pénétrant l'*endroit* qu'il veut, ou mieux, si l'auteur a su ce qu'il voulut, le vrai décor exosmosé sur la scène. L'écriteau apporté selon les changements de lieu évite le rappel périodique au non-esprit par le changement des décors matériels, que l'on perçoit surtout à l'instant de leur différence.

"Dans ces conditions, toute partie de décor dont on aura un besoin spécial, fenêtre qu'on ouvre, porte qu'on enfonce, est un accessoire et peut être apportée comme une table ou un flambeau." — *Œuvres complètes,* v. 4, pp. 161–167.

35. *Ibid.,* p. 167.

36. Quoted in Walter Tritsch, "Thornton Wilder in Berlin," *Living Age,* CCCXLI (September, 1931), 45 f.

37. "Joyce and the Modern Novel," pp. 14 f.

38. *Ibid.,* p. 15.

39. Uncatalogued "Author's suggestions for staging the play," Yale Collection of American Literature.

40. Memo on second half of Act I, *The Skin of Our Teeth,* p. 4, in the possession of Mr. Wilder.

41. *The Skin of Our Teeth,* p. 121.

42. *Three Plays,* p. xii.

IV: CHARACTERIZATION AND NARRATION

1. Thornton Wilder, "Some Thoughts on Playwriting," in Augusto Centeno, ed., *The Intent of the Artist* (Princeton, 1941), p. 97.

2. Gertrude Stein, *Narration* (Chicago, 1935), p. 61.

3. " 'Our Town' — From Stage to Screen," *Theatre Arts,* XXIV (November, 1940), 824.

4. *Ibid.,* p. 876.

5. *Ibid.,* pp. 817 f.

6. *Ibid.,* p. 818.

7. Uncatalogued letter to Max Reinhardt, Yale Library Collection of American Literature.

8. Thornton Wilder, "Noting the Nature of Farce," source not known, in the possession of Mr. Wilder.

9. *Ibid.*

10. See Appendix for parallel passages of *The Merchant of Yonkers* and *L'Avare.*

11. Molière, *Théâtre,* v. 4 (Paris, 1949), p. 133.

12. Thornton Wilder, *The Merchant of Yonkers* (New York, 1939), p. 30.

13. "Of Sedition and Troubles," *The Works of Sir Francis Bacon,* v. 1 (Philadelphia, 1854), p. 23.

14. *The Merchant of Yonkers,* p. 50.

15. Thornton Wilder, *The Skin of Our Teeth,* in *Three Plays* (New York, 1957), p. 191.

16. *The Merchant of Yonkers,* p. 172.

17. *Ibid.,* pp. 173 f.

18. *The Skin of Our Teeth,* p. 110.

19. Uncatalogued letter from Tallulah Bankhead to Michael Meyer-

berg, dated October 28, 1942, Yale Library Collection of American Literature.

20. Typescript of *The Alcestiad,* in the possession of Mr. Wilder, pp. 1:16 f.

21. David Grene and Richmond Lattimore, *The Complete Greek Tragedies,* v. III, *Euripides* (Chicago, 1959), p. 270.

22. Stark Young, "Mei Lan-fang," *New Republic,* LXII (March 5, 1930), 74.

23. Thornton Wilder, "A Preface for 'Our Town,'" *New York Times,* February 13, 1938, sec. 2, p. 1.

24. "Mei Lan-fang," p. 75.

25. "Some Thoughts on Playwriting," p. 94.

26. Richard Boleslavsky, *Acting, The First Six Lessons* (New York, 1933), pp. 97 f.

27. "Some Thoughts on Playwriting," p. 89.

28. *Acting, The First Six Lessons,* p. 82.

29. *Ibid.,* p. 83.

30. *Ibid.,* p. 84.

31. "Some Thoughts on Playwriting," p. 85.

32. *Ibid.,* p. 86.

33. *Ibid.,* p. 87.

34. *Narration,* pp. 18 f.

35. *Ibid.,* p. 22.

36. Malcolm Cowley, ed., *Writers at Work* (New York, 1958), pp. 105 f.

37. Quoted in Ross Parmenter, "Novelist into Playwright," *Saturday Review of Literature,* XVIII (June 11, 1938), 10.

V: AN AMERICAN LANGUAGE

1. Thornton Wilder, *The Angel That Troubled the Waters* (New York, 1928), p. xiv.

2. *Ibid.,* pp. xv f.

3. *Ibid.*

4. Jacques Maritain, *Creative Intuition in Art and Poetry* (New York, 1933), p. 133.

5. Gertrude Stein, *Lectures in America* (New York, 1935), p. 201.

6. Thornton Wilder, "Toward an American Language," *Atlantic,* CXC (July, 1952), 31.

7. *Lectures in America,* pp. 49 f.

8. *Ibid.*, p. 161.

9. *Ibid.*, p. 183.

10. "Toward an American Language," p. 32.

11. *Lectures in America*, p. 51.

12. *Ibid.*, pp. 53 f.

13. *Ibid.*, pp. 95–110.

14. *Ibid.*, pp. 118 f.

15. *Ibid.*, p. 125.

16. "Toward an American Language," p. 33.

17. Gertrude Stein, *Four in America* (New Haven, 1947), p. viii.

18. *Lectures in America*, p. 147.

19. *Four in America*, p. xi.

20. Malcolm Cowley, ed., *Writers at Work* (New York, 1958), p. 108.

21. *Lectures in America*, pp. 40 f.

22. "Toward an American Language," p. 30.

23. *Ibid.*

24. Thornton Wilder, *Lucrece, from "Le Viol de Lucrèce" by André Obey* (Boston and New York, 1933), p. 73.

25. Stark Young, "Sorrow's Sharp Sustaining," *New Republic,* CXXIII (January 18, 1933), 268.

26. *Ibid.*

27. Gertrude Stein, *The Making of Americans* (New York, 1934), p. 38.

28. Thornton Wilder, "The Warship," *Yale Literary Magazine,* CI (February, 1936), 66.

29. Whit Burnett, ed., *This Is My Best* (New York, 1942), p. 762.

30. Cowley, *Writers at Work,* p. 112.

31. Thornton Wilder, *The Long Christmas Dinner* (New Haven, 1931), p. 37.

32. "Toward an American Language," p. 37.

33. *Ibid.*

34. *Ibid.*, p. 34.

35. *Lectures in America*, p. 165.

36. *Ibid.*

37. "Toward an American Language," p. 34.

38. *Lectures in America*, pp. 167 f.

39. Typescript of "L'Œuvre et le langage," in the possession of Mr. Wilder, pp. 2 f.

40. Thornton Wilder, *The Skin of Our Teeth,* in *Three Plays* (New York, 1957), pp. 193 f.

41. "Toward an American Language," p. 33.

42. Typescript of *The Alcestiad,* in the possession of Mr. Wilder, p. 213.

43. "Toward an American Language," p. 31.

44. *Ibid.,* p. 34.

45. "L'Œuvre et le langage," p. 2.

46. *Lectures in America,* p. 233.

47. *Ibid.,* pp. 209 f.

48. *Ibid.,* p. 233.

49. *Ibid.,* p. 237.

50. *Ibid.,* p. 214.

51. "Toward an American Language," p. 36.

52. *Ibid.,* p. 37.

53. *Lectures in America,* p. 209.

VI: MYTH

1. Malcolm Cowley, ed., *Writers at Work* (New York, 1958), p. 109.

2. Richard Beer-Hofmann, *Jacob's Dream* (New York, 1946), p. xvi.

3. *Ibid.,* p. xiii.

4. Thornton Wilder, "Joyce and the Modern Novel," *A James Joyce Miscellany* (n.p., 1957), p. 15.

5. *Ibid.*

6. Joseph Campbell and Henry Morton Robinson, "The Skin of Whose Teeth?," *Saturday Review of Literature,* XXV (December 19, 1942), 3–4, and "The Skin of Whose Teeth?: Part II," *Saturday Review of Literature,* XXVI (February 13, 1943), 16–19.

7. Henry Morton Robinson, "The Curious Case of Thornton Wilder," *Esquire,* XLVII (March, 1957), 70–71, 124, 125, 126.

8. Edmund Wilson, "The Antrobuses and the Earwickers," *Nation,* CXVI (January 30, 1943), 167 f.

9. Robert van Gelder, "Interview with a Best-Selling Author: Thornton Wilder," *Cosmopolitan,* CXXIV (April, 1948), 120.

10. "The Skin of Whose Teeth?," p. 3.

11. Theodore Dreiser, *Plays of the Natural and the Supernatural* (New York, 1916), p. 107.

12. *Ibid.,* p. 109.

13. *Ibid.*, p. 110.

14. *Ibid.*

15. *Ibid.*, p. 112.

16. Thornton Wilder, "World Literature and the Modern Mind," in Arnold Bergstraesser, ed., *Goethe and the Modern Age* (Chicago, 1950), p. 218.

17. Norman Holmes Pearson, "The American Novelist and the Uses of Europe," *Some American Studies* (Kyoto, 1964).

18. Ezra Pound is one of the two modern American writers whom Wilder admires and to whom he feels indebted. See Cowley, *Writers at Work*, p. 115.

19. Beer-Hofmann, *Jacob's Dream*, p. xi.

20. *Ibid.*

21. *Ibid.*, p. xii.

22. André Maurois, *A Private Universe*, tr. Hamish Miles (New York, 1932), p. 39.

23. "The American Novelist and the Uses of Europe," p. 18.

24. S. Kierkegaard, *Fear and Trembling*, tr. Walter Lowrie (Princeton, 1941), p. 87.

25. Thornton Wilder, "The American Loneliness," *Atlantic*, CXC (August, 1952), 66.

26. *Fear and Trembling*, p. 88.

27. *Ibid.*, p. 91.

28. *Ibid.*, p. 93.

29. Thornton Wilder, "Emily Dickinson," *Atlantic*, CXC (November, 1952), 47 f.

30. *Ibid.*

31. My translation. The original is:

"Kultur in einer Demokratie hat ihre Gefahren — aber auch eine Aufgabe und eine Verheissung.

"Ihr eroeffnet sich ein neues ungeheures Thema, das zu beschreiben, das mit Denken zu durchdringen, das auszudruecken und das zu erforschen ist: Der Mensch erhobenen Hauptes.

"Diese Haltung und dieser Anspruch sind zunaechst verwirrend, wie uns Werke der Literatur in den letzen Jahren gezeigt haben; sie koennen sogar in die Verzweiflung fuehren.

"Die Demokratie hat eine grosse Aufgabe: Naemlich neue Mythen, neue Metaphern und neue Bilder zu schaffen und den neuen Stand der Wuerde aufzuzeigen, in den der Mensch getreten ist." — Thornton Wilder, *Kultur in einer Demokratie* (Frankfurt-am-Main, 1957), p. 8.

APPENDIX

1. Thornton Wilder, *The Merchant of Yonkers* (New York, 1939), pp. 32–34.

2. Molière, *Théâtre,* v. 4 (Paris, 1949), pp. 82–84.

3. Wilder, pp. 36–38.

4. Molière, pp. 85–87.

5. Wilder, pp. 38–39.

6. Molière, pp. 84–85.

7. Wilder, pp. 40–41.

8. Molière, pp. 87–89.

BIBLIOGRAPHY

I. *The Works of Thornton Wilder:*

A. *Manuscripts and Typescripts*

The Alcestiad, typescript, in the possession of Mr. Wilder.

A Doll's House, by Henrik Ibsen, typescript, in a new acting version by Thornton Wilder, in the possession of Mr. Wilder.

The Happy Journey to Trenton and Camden, manuscript, Yale Library Collection of American Literature.

"L'Œuvre et le langage," typescript, in the possession of Mr. Wilder.

Our Town, first full manuscript, only Acts I and III, Yale Library Collection of American Literature.

Our Town, second full manuscript, only Act I, Yale Library Collection of American Literature.

Our Town, first full typescript, Acts I, II, and III, Yale Library Collection of American Literature.

"Pride: Bernice," typescript, in the possession of Mr. Wilder.

The Sea Gull, by Anton Chekov, changes and additions in dialogue by Thornton Wilder, Yale Library Collection of American Literature.

Sloth: the Wreck on the Five-Twenty-Five, typescript, in the possession of Mr. Wilder.

The Woman of Andros, manuscript, Yale Library Collection of American Literature.

B. *Plays*

"The Trumpet Shall Sound . . . Act One," *Yale Literary Magazine,* LXXXV (October, 1919), 9-26.

"The Trumpet Shall Sound . . . Act Two," *Yale Literary Magazine,* LXXXV (November, 1919), 78-92.

"The Trumpet Shall Sound . . . Act Three," *Yale Literary Magazine,* LXXXV (December, 1919), 128-146.

"The Trumpet Shall Sound . . . Act Four," *Yale Literary Magazine,* LXXXV (January, 1920), 192–207.

The Angel That Troubled the Waters (New York, 1928).

The Long Christmas Dinner and Other Plays (New York and New Haven, 1931).

Lucrece (Boston and New York, 1933).

Our Town (New York, 1938).

The Merchant of Yonkers (New York and London, 1939).

The Skin of Our Teeth (New York and London, 1942).

Our Century (n.p., 1947).

Three Plays (New York, 1957), contains *The Matchmaker,* a revision of *The Merchant of Yonkers,* as well as *Our Town* and *The Skin of Our Teeth.*

"The Drunken Sisters," *Atlantic,* CC (November, 1957), 92–95.

"Childhood," *Atlantic,* CVI (November, 1960), 78–84.

Die Alkestiade, tr. Herberth E. Herlitschka (Frankfurt-am-Main and Hamburg), 1960.

C. *Fiction*

The Cabala (New York, 1926).

The Bridge of San Luis Rey (New York, 1927).

The Woman of Andros (New York, 1930).

Heaven's My Destination (London, New York, and Toronto, 1934).

"The Warship," *Yale Literary Magazine,* CI (February, 1936), 64–67.

The Ides of March (New York and London, 1948).

D. *Nonfiction*

"Playgoing Nights," *Theatre Arts,* XIII (June, 1929), 411–419. Written by Thornton Wilder and his sister Isabel Wilder.

TRITSCH, WALTER, "Thornton Wilder in Berlin," *Living Age,* CCCXLI (September, 1931), 44–47. This interview appeared earlier in *Die Literarische Welt,* VII (June 12, 1931), 1–2.

MAUROIS, ANDRÉ, *A Private Universe,* tr. Hamish Miles (New York, 1932). Contains quotations from conversation with Thornton Wilder, August 18, 1928, pp. 38–41.

STEIN, GERTRUDE, *Narration* (Chicago, 1935). Introduction, pp. v–viii, by Thornton Wilder.

———, *The Geographical History of America* (n.p., 1936). Introduction, pp. 7–14, by Thornton Wilder.

" 'Our Town' — From Stage to Screen," *Theatre Arts,* XXIV (November, 1940), 815–824. Correspondence between Thornton Wilder and Sol Lesser about the production of *Our Town.*

"James Joyce," *Poetry, A Magazine of Verse,* LVII (March, 1941), 370–374. Reprinted as a pamphlet (Aurora, N.Y., 1944).

"Some Thoughts on Playwriting," *The Intent of the Artist,* ed. AUGUSTO CENTENO (Princeton, 1941), pp. 83–98.

BEER-HOFMANN, RICHARD, *Jacob's Dream* (New York, 1946). Introduction, pp. xi–xviii, by Thornton Wilder.

STEIN, GERTRUDE, *Four in America* (New Haven, 1947). Introduction, pp. v–xxvii, by Thornton Wilder.

"World Literature and the Modern Mind," *Goethe and the Modern Age,* ed. ARNOLD BERGSTRAESSER (Chicago, 1950), pp. 213–224.

"Thoughts for Our Times," *Harvard Alumni Bulletin,* LIII (July 7, 1951), 779–781.

"A Time of Troubles," *Academy Papers,* Addresses on the Evangeline Wilbour Blashfield Foundation, v. 2 (New York, 1951), pp. 218–220.

"New Aids toward Dating the Early Plays of Lope de Vega," *Varia Variorum* (Münster, 1952), pp. 194–200.

"Toward an American Language," *Atlantic,* CXC (July, 1952), 29–37. This and the following two essays were part of Mr. Wilder's Charles Eliot Norton lectures at Harvard in 1950–1951.

"The American Loneliness," *Atlantic,* CXC (August, 1952), 65–69.

"Emily Dickinson," *Atlantic,* CXC (November, 1952), 43–48.

"Exploration and Explanation," *Seventy-five* (New Haven, 1953), pp. 76–77.

"Silent Generation," *Harpers,* CCVI (April, 1953), 34–36.

GALLUP, DONALD, ed., *The Flowers of Friendship* (New York, 1953). Contains five letters from Thornton Wilder to Gertrude Stein and Alice B. Toklas, pp. 303–307, 336–337, 338–339.

"Lope, Pinedo, Some Child-Actors, and a Lion," *Romance Philology,* VII (August, 1953), 19–25.

"General Report," *The Artist in Modern Society* (n.p., 1954), pp. 121–124.

SOPHOCLES, *Oedipus the King,* tr. Francis Storr (New York, 1955). Introduction, pp. 9–20, by Thornton Wilder.

BARNES, ERIC WOLLENCOTT, *The Man Who Lived Twice* (New York, 1956). Excerpts from five letters from Thornton Wilder to Edward Sheldon, pp. 177, 219–222, and three comments by Wilder about Sheldon, pp. 219, 264, 320.

"Joyce and the Modern Novel," *A James Joyce Miscellany* (n.p., 1957), pp. 11–19.

"The Art of Fiction XVI," *Paris Review* (Winter, 1957), pp. 37–57. Reprinted in Malcolm Cowley, ed., *Writers at Work* (New York, 1958), pp. 99–118.

"A Platform and a Passion or Two," *Harpers,* CCXV (October, 1957), 48–51.

Kultur in einer Demokratie (Frankfurt-am-Main), 1957.

II. *A Selection of Works about Thornton Wilder*

Brown, E. K., "Christian Humanist: Thornton Wilder," *University of Toronto Quarterly,* IV (April, 1935), 356–370.

Burbank, Rex, *Thornton Wilder* (New York, 1961).

Campbell, Joseph, and Henry Morton Robinson, "The Skin of Whose Teeth?", *Saturday Review of Literature,* XXV (December 19, 1942), 3–4.

———, "The Skin of Whose Teeth?: Part II," *Saturday Review of Literature,* XXVI (February 13, 1943), 16–19.

Clurman, Harold, "Theater," *Nation,* CLXXXI (September 3, 1955), 210.

Cowley, Malcolm, "The Man Who Abolished Time," *Saturday Review of Literature,* XXXIX (October 6, 1956), 13–14, 50, 51, 52. Reprinted in a slightly different form as introduction to: Thornton Wilder, *A Thornton Wilder Trio* (New York, 1956), pp. 1–19.

Edelstein, J. M., *A Bibliographical Checklist of the Writings of Thornton Wilder* (New Haven, 1959).

Fergusson, Francis, "Three Allegorists: Brecht, Wilder and Eliot," *Sewanee Review,* LXIV (Fall, 1956), 544–573. Reprinted in: Francis Fergusson, *The Human Image in Dramatic Literature* (Garden City), pp. 41–47.

Firebaugh, Joseph J., "The Humanism of Thornton Wilder," *Pacific Spectator,* IV (Autumn, 1950), 426–438.

Fuller, E., "Thornton Wilder: The Notation of the Heart," *American Scholar,* XXVIII (Spring, 1959), 210–217.

Gold, Michael, "Wilder: Prophet of the Genteel Christ," *New Republic,* LXIV (October 22, 1930), 266–267.

Kosok, Heinz, "Thornton Wilder: A Bibliography of Criticism," *Twentieth Century Literature,* IX (1963), 93–100.

MILLER, ARTHUR, "The Family in Modern Drama," *Atlantic*, CXCVII (April, 1956), 35–41.

"An Obliging Man," *Time*, LXI (January 12, 1953), 44–49.

PAPAJEWSKI, HELMUT, *Thornton Wilder* (Frankfurt-am-Main and Bonn, 1961).

PARMENTER, ROSS, "Novelist into Playwright," *Saturday Review of Literature*, XVIII (June 11, 1938), 10–11.

ROBINSON, HENRY MORTON, "The Curious Case of Thornton Wilder," *Esquire*, XLVII (March, 1957), 70–71, 124, 125, 126.

STRESAU, HERMAN, *Thornton Wilder* (Berlin, 1963).

ULRICH, DOROTHY, "Thornton Wilder: Professor and Playwright," *University of Chicago Magazine*, n.v. (April, 1938), 7–9.

VAN GELDER, ROBERT, "Interview with a Best-Selling Author: Thornton Wilder," *Cosmopolitan*, CXXIV (April, 1948), 18, 120, 121, 122, 123.

WEALES, GERALD, "Unfashionable Optimist," *Commonweal*, LXVII (February 7, 1958), 486–488.

INDEX